What people are saying
100 Action Principles

I read the *100 Action Principles of the Shaolin* with great interest. The principles described in the book are ones that everyone can truly take to heart and benefit from. Finding inner peace is the key to a person's happiness. Only with inner peace can we develop the mental and physical strength needed to handle the rigors of today's fast paced life.

Congratulations on your success and national recognition for offering free business education on the Internet. On behalf of the people of Guam, I wish you the best of luck in all your endeavors.

Carl T.C. Gutierrez, Governor of Guam

What a great little book! It's easy to carry around and one can refer to it at any time.

US Representative Cliff Stearns

Having a copy of this means a great deal to me and will certainly come in handy. It will have a special place in my library.

US Senator Michael B. Enzi

A sincere thank-you for the book.

Lincoln Almond, Governor of Rhode Island

Thank you so much. I am intrigued by the book.

Frank O'Bannon, Governor of Indiana

A wonderful addition to my collection.

E. Benjamin Nelson, Governor of Nebraska

This book is thoughtful and hard hitting, and if you follow through will lead you to a better life.

Bill Rogers, Olympian

A great inspirational guide for daily living and personal success.

Dan R. Bannister, CEO DynCorp

Really good stuff.

James J. Howard, CEO, Northern States Power

I loved it. I could not stop going from page to page reminding myself why I decided to study Shaolin Karate.

Jeanne Crowley, Black Belt

It impresses me as a useful quick reference guide for personal and business use.

David L. Squier, CEO, Howmet Corp.

I was so psyched after reading this book. I think it is great and all the Black Belts that I meet feel the same way.

Pam Smith, 3rd Degree Black Belt

Very interesting, informative and helpful.

Manuel Avendando, Managing Editor,
El Diario La Prensa

I thought so much of this motivational book that I've passed it out to many students and friends, and it is having a rippling effect.

Jeanne Friswell, 3rd Degree Black Belt.

Congratulations. Common sense values condensed in any easy read.

Gerald Lestina, CEO, Roundy's Corp

Packs a wealth of wisdom for life.

Dr. Robert Doherty

This small book is big on the secrets of life. It's a must read. I've given copies to my son and daughter.

Bob Thompson, 4th Degree Black Belt

A very enlightening, pleasurable experience. I recommend the book to all my students.

Kenneth Loyer, 3rd Degree Black Belt

The book is enjoyable and very easy to read. The ideas are common sense, but enlightening at the same time.

Brian Hoey, 4th Degree Black Belt

An invaluable resource for the martial artist and business person alike. This book will inspire anyone trying to succeed in business and in life.

Morris Collins, 2nd Degree Black Belt.

As the book states "Everyone has all the answers within." This book helps bring them out.

Rick Boiardi, 2nd Degree Black Belt

You know, there's an old Chinese proverb that states, "The longest journey starts with but a single step!," a simple yet profound observation. Bill, your book, *100 Action Principles of the Shaolin* helps simplify the long journey of life. Reading your book is like being in a room with one hundred mirrors. You show one hundred simplified, easy ways to look at oneself internally and externally, and evaluate what we look like, and what direction we're heading. The references in the book to the martial arts are especially interesting to me, because the one hundred principles, like the application of martial arts, are a life-long learning experience. The book was fun to read. Good things do come in small packages.

Arnold Goldstein, 3rd Degree Black Belt.

I will keep re-reading the book. It is a great guide to happiness and success.

Dean L. Buntrock, CEO WMX Technologies

A helpful and informative book ... with the capacity to assist me in my public as well as my private life.

US Senator John Ashcroft

The principles taught are the cornerstone for success in business and personal life. By closely adhering to the principles one can be on track to achieve their desired success.

Jeffrey Prag, Businessman

100 Action Principles of the Shaolin

By Bill FitzPatrick
The Shaolin Master™

100 ACTION PRINCIPLES OF THE SHAOLIN. Copyright © 1997, 1998 (Second edition) by the American Success Institute, Inc. All rights reserved. No part of this book may be reproduced or transmitted in any form or by any means, electronic or mechanical, including photocopying, recording, or by any information storage and retrieval system, without permission in writing from the American Success Institute, Inc.

POSITIVE MENTAL ATTITUDES™, AFRICAN-AMERICANS ON SUCCESS™, SPORTS LEGENDS ON SUCCESS™, WINNING WITH SMALL BUSINESS™, TENGA UNA ACTITUD MENTAL POSITIVA™, WOMEN ON SUCCESS™, SPORTS LEGENDS ON SUCCESS™ and ATTITUDES MENTALES POSITIVES™ are all trademarks of the American Success Institute, Inc.

Educational and motivational materials from the American Success Institute are available at special discounts for bulk purchases. For additional information, contact:

American Success Institute

5 North Main Street

Natick, MA 01760

www.success.org

Phone: 508-651-3303

e-mail: info@success.org

Cover, book design, typography, and electronic pagination by Painted Turtle Productions, Newton, MA. www.paintedturtle.com

Printed in the United States of America

ISBN 1-884864-10-4

Library of Congress Catalog Card Number 98-71368

Table of Contents

A Personal Message From Bill FitzPatrick

What is so inviting about the tried and true advice of the Shaolin action principles is that the beneficial results are immediate. You don't have to spend a year in graduate school, two days fasting or an hour chanting. You can make an immediate conscious decision to listen more, to smile more, to be more patient, to learn and to use people's names more, to take the initiative more. These types of immediate actions yield immediate positive results.

The tone of the action principles is motivational. It is *can do*. It is challenging. This book is for you, a person of action willing to study and work hard for yourself and your family. As you begin to fulfill your own personal and financial goals, you will find that you will have the resources, time and peace of mind to share your good fortune and positive attitude with others. Your life will evolve from making a living to making a difference.

I hope that in thinking about the principles, you will come to the realization that you already know most of what you need to know to achieve success in self-defense, business and life. The same rules apply. These are the same rules that have always applied to successful living throughout history and across cultures. You already know that success takes persistence, determination and hard work. You already know that success requires objectives and goals formulated in a clearly defined plan. Simply put, the secrets to success aren't secret. We already know what to do. We already possess the God given inner qualities. Now, we must each make a conscious decision to act.

Let's begin.

About the Shaolin Action Principles

This book offers the example of the Shaolin monk as a model for successful living in the twenty-first century. Fifteen hundred years ago, legend has it that the Shaolin monks served their people as warriors and priests. They were men of action ready to defend and men of peace ready to console.

The Shaolin monk as warrior was disciplined, brave, adaptable and action oriented.

The Shaolin monk as priest was kind, generous, intelligent and service oriented.

By choosing the Shaolin monks as our model, we are choosing to be disciplined and kind, brave and generous, adaptable and intelligent, and both action and service oriented. Immediately, by assuming these character traits we stand a good chance of being more successful in business and in our personal relationships. We commit ourselves to positive action. It isn't easy but we will try day to day. We can say *Yes* to a life dedicated to personal achievement, protection and service.

In the Shaolin philosophy, the monk and the warrior can exist as one. The Shaolin warrior doesn't attack. The Shaolin warrior seeks peace and harmony. If he receives a punch or kick, he merely returns that punch or kick to the attacker.

The Shaolin action principles are not religious principles. The Shaolin action principles present a simple philosophical outlook on how to live harmoniously yet comfortably in the modern world. They are more directed toward finding inner peace than about the small issue of physical fighting. The principles evolve from the important lessons to be learned from self-reliance. The Shaolin action principles offer us a perspective to assess where we are and where we hope to go. You will find many time tested motivational maxims embedded in the principles.

The Shaolin action principles should help us to develop a mental and physical toughness to handle the rigors of everyday living as we work toward our goals.

The Shaolin action principles should help to develop a mental and physical softness expressed in an inner peace from the knowledge that we are putting forth our best effort.

The Shaolin action principles are short bits of action oriented advice that can guide us in our lifelong quest for spiritual and mental growth, health and financial prosperity.

The Shaolin Legend

The first Shaolin temple was built on Wu Tai Mountain in Honan Province in Northern China around 370 AD. The word Shaolin translates from the Mandarin Chinese for new or young forest. It was here that the Shaolin martial arts were begun in the sixth century by Bodhidharma, a travelling Buddhist monk from India.

Bodhidharma taught the monks that enlightenment, God, came from within and not from outside gods. To find this inner enlightenment, the monks would meditate in a sedentary position for many hours. This practice made them spiritually strong and physically weak. To keep the monks healthy, Bodhidharma began to teach them *Chi Kung* which is based on Indian yoga. *Chi* means energy and *kung* means work. These *Chi Kung* exercises formed the basis for the Shaolin martial arts. The first *kata* or form that Bodhidharma taught was called the Eighteen Lohan consisting only of hand motions.

In addition to their Temple chores, young monks attended a series of two-hour training sessions each day. Junior students attended three such sessions. Senior students received a fourth midnight class. To be regarded as a martial arts master and to leave the Temple as a Shaolin warrior-monk, a student had to defend himself at each of five gates that were guarded by his teachers.

By the seventh century, over one thousand monks lived at the Shaolin Temple. The Shaolin monks were allowed to exist at the sufferance of the emperor who on occasion used the monks to put down civil unrest.

The warrior monks travelled extensively ministering to those they met, setting up new temples and accepting novices to learn the martial arts. Some monks found their way to Korea and Japan where they served as teachers, bodyguards and spiritual leaders.

The original Shaolin temple was destroyed in the early 1920s. It was rebuilt in the 1950s and is today a popular tourist destination.

Today, the Shaolin style, as with most of the martial arts taught outside of Asia, has evolved into an eclectic blend of traditional Chinese and Japanese techniques combined with modern self-defense applications.

How To Use This Book

Following the Shaolin action principles can help you make positive changes in your life. However, you must do more than read. This book is a call to action. The principles will encourage you to take immediate actions that will have immediate positive rewards which, in turn, will motivate you to continue using them and teaching them to others. You do not have to be a martial artist to benefit from the Shaolin action principles.

Read. Consider. Act.

The principles have been randomly ordered. There is no priority. Read one. If it sounds interesting, try it out. Pick and choose as you create your own personal success philosophy; your own goals; your own plan of action.

What business? Any. What education? Your own. What do you need? Nothing besides this guide and your commitment to self-reliance. When to start? Now.

You can make this choice.

If you agree with most of the action principles, you will like our website at www.success.org, where themes on positive living are more fully developed. It's all FREE.

If you appreciate this book, consider making a donation to the American Success Institute and helping us to distribute copies of the book to your fellow students, employees, customers and members of your community. Call 1-800-585-1300 for details.

About www.success.org

Success.org is the national award-winning website of the American Success Institute. On the site, you will find valuable information on entrepreneurship, investments and personal development. You will find books, courses, articles, stories, resources and thousands of quotes to give you the inspiration and motivation to become a person of action and to live your dreams. If you like this book, you will enjoy using the educational materials offered at www.success.org. It's all FREE. Take advantage of this site and let others know about success.org.

A journey of a thousand miles begins with a single step.

Lao-tzu, 600 B.C.,
The Way of Lao-tzu

1

Set Goals

You will either shape your life, or circumstance will shape your life for you. For which results will you plan, work, sacrifice, invest, persist?

You are the sculptor. You create your own image. Have others already done what it is that you want to do? Study them and do what they did. Start anywhere at anytime and persist.

In the beginning, don't be too concerned about how you will achieve your goals. With commitment, research and patience, the means will come. Your goals will evolve into a set of action oriented objectives. The objectives become a series of to-dos. Every day, you do what's on your to-do list. You reach the objectives and eventually obtain the goal.

Write your goals down. Visualize the attainment of your goals often. Goals are dreams with dates attached. Commit yourself by sharing your goals with others. Every day, you're one day closer. You will only become as great as the goals you choose. Decide today where you will end up. Think BIG.

The best victory is when the opponent surrenders of its own accord before there are any actual hostilities... It is best to win without fighting.

Sun-tzu, 400 B.C.
The Art of War

Develop Winning Strategies

Begin by clearly focusing on your objectives. Exactly what do you want to accomplish? How have other people dealt with similar objectives? Can you do what they did? There is no point in re-inventing the wheel. If a proven strategy already exists, find it and try it.

Choose the best option. Consider alternative strategies if your original option doesn't work or needs to be compromised. If you are daring, some of your ideas aren't going to work. Adapt. Try something else. Keep trying. Keep taking action.

Don't just invent new strategies for invention's sake. If an ad works, stick with the ad. If an offer to attract new students is bringing in new students, keep the same offer. In the martial arts or in business, if a technique works, stick with the technique. Develop winning strategies and keep those that prove effective. If you have one kick and it always works, that's great. If you have one product and you can keep selling it, that's great.

He that is afraid to throw the dice will never roll a six.

Chinese proverb

3

Be Decisive

You want to make enough money so that you can retire early and spend your time developing your human potential and helping others. If you follow the Shaolin action principles, this can be done if you behave decisively.

Prepare your goals and objectives. Devote yourself to research and hard work. Find mentors and form alliances. Seek quality and commit to customer service. Keep changing until you find your way.

While you are building your asset base, live frugally, save and invest.

Keep yourself fit while enjoying the benefits of martial arts training.

If you observe martial artists in action, you will notice that they will shout as they execute various moves. This shout is called a *kiai*. The *kiai* is the forced breath signifying that all of the fighter's energy is being concentrated on the application of a technique. It's decisive action.

Make up your mind to be a success and then do it. From this moment on, be decisive.

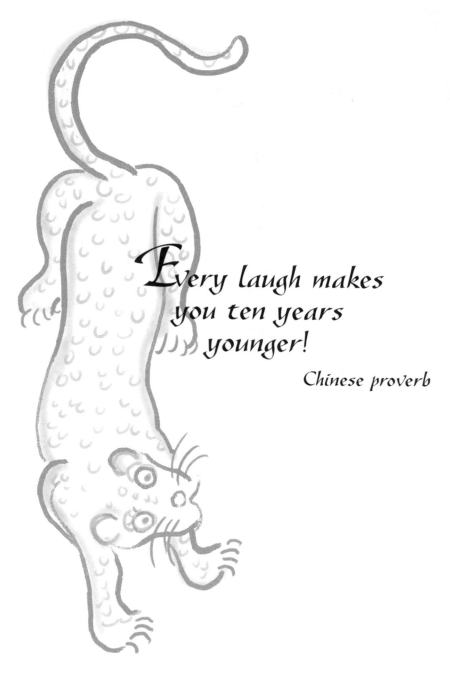

Every laugh makes
you ten years
younger!

Chinese proverb

Maintain A Positive Attitude

Get up, stretch and be happy because today you are one day closer to your goals. You know who you are and where you are going. You are generous and kind and hard working. Above all, you are self-reliant. You know that success can be yours because success is in your own hands. You feel the enlivening power of having control over your own future. You expect good things to happen. Optimism is a wonderful feeling.

You are your thoughts. You are thankful for being tough enough to take a few setbacks and keep going forward. You are thankful to have the curiosity to keep learning. You are thankful to see opportunity knock so often. You are thankful to have the personality to keep making new friends. Your mind can only hold one thought at a time so make that one thought positive.

One of the five Shaolin animals is the dragon. The dragon possesses many different techniques to deal with opponents. The spirit of the dragon is indomitable. He cannot be destroyed. The dragon is the Shaolin symbol for heaven.

You are a positive thinker for whom all is a possibility. Count your blessings. The way is clear. You are a follower of the Shaolin principles. The world is a better place because you are in it. See the motivational resources section at www.success.org.

The outstanding
characteristic of the expert
athlete is his ease of
movement, even during
maximal effort.
You are never set or
tensed, but ready
and flexible.

Bruce Lee, 1975,
Tao of Jeet Kune Do

5
Relax Your Body

When a martial artist delivers a punch or kick, the object is to remain loose and light. This aids speed and focus. The only time that rigid force is needed in karate is when contact is made. Most karate movements are loose, light, fluid, agile and flexible, rather than tense, hard, rigid and stiff.

The martial artist realizes that although he may be young and powerful today he must prepare for tomorrow when he will be neither. If he relied on brute strength alone, it would follow that he would become a less efficient warrior as he aged and became physically weaker. The martial artist accepts that in addition to continued strength training, he must also work on endurance, speed, agility, timing and coordination.

All opponents cannot be defeated through head charging confrontation. As the martial artist reaches the black belt level, he learns an ever increasing number of physical and mental techniques to deal with opponents. The martial arts offer a lifetime learning opportunity.

In your personal dealings, remain loose and light. Eliminate stress. There is rarely need to be tense and hard-headed. Many fights can be won and problems solved with calm reason and a soft voice.

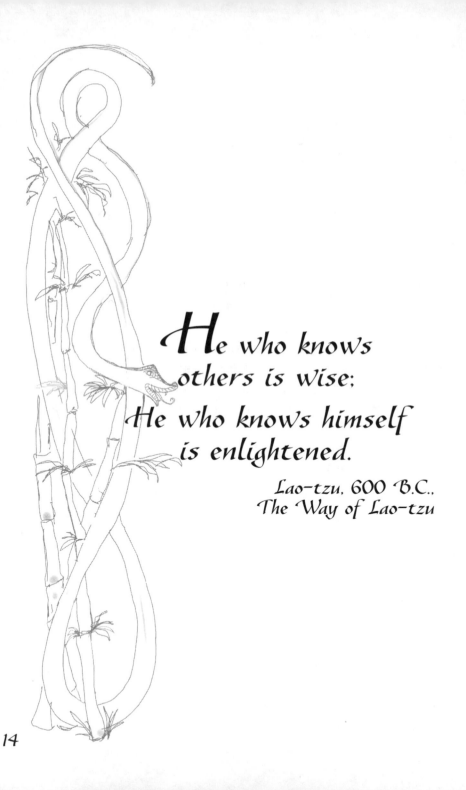

He who knows
others is wise;
He who knows himself
is enlightened.

Lao-tzu, 600 B.C.,
The Way of Lao-tzu

6
Look in the Mirror

Look at yourself as your family, co-workers, customers, students and the general public may be seeing you. Endeavor to like and admire what you and they see.

Don't kid yourself and fall victim to self-deception. You can't honestly judge others if you can't honestly judge yourself. You cannot build a stronger self if you rely upon what may be the self-serving false appraisal and expectations of others. Do yourself a favor and be honest with yourself. Are you doing all you can do? If you are not honest with yourself, you will be haunted by doubts and fears.

To keep yourself on the correct course to accomplishing your goals, subject your attitudes and actions to constant review. During your quiet time each day, quickly contemplate the thought: Is this the way that I want to be thinking and acting? Make self-reflection a daily habit. Pay close attention to yourself.

The essence of
karate is the
spirit, the unity
of body and
soul.

Shihan Tak Kubota, 1977,
The Art of Karate

7
Enjoy Your Own Company

Everyone needs quiet time in their day when they can just be with their own thoughts. This isn't daydreaming. The serenity of quiet time can be enjoyed in a variety of ways. It can be traditional Zen or TM type meditation, but it can also be taking a walk, gardening, making a pot of tea or taking a long, hot shower. You may wish to pray. Each day, take twenty minutes to stop, reflect and enjoy being who you are. Think about the past, present, future or nothing in particular. Relax by yourself and you will feel renewed. Tranquillity will re-energize you. Without trying, you will be amazed at how your subconscious mind releases so many good ideas.

Just as the time you spend in the *dojo* (the martial arts training center) or gym strengthens the physical you, quiet reflection strengthens the spiritual you. Quiet time also gives you the opportunity to practice minding your own business.

Take a deep breath and continue to breathe slowly and steadily. Look around. Use all your senses. You will find contentment in the solitude. If you follow the Shaolin action principles, you can be proud of the way that you live. Your life is significant. See Lesson #12 of the Winning With Small Business Course at www.success.org.

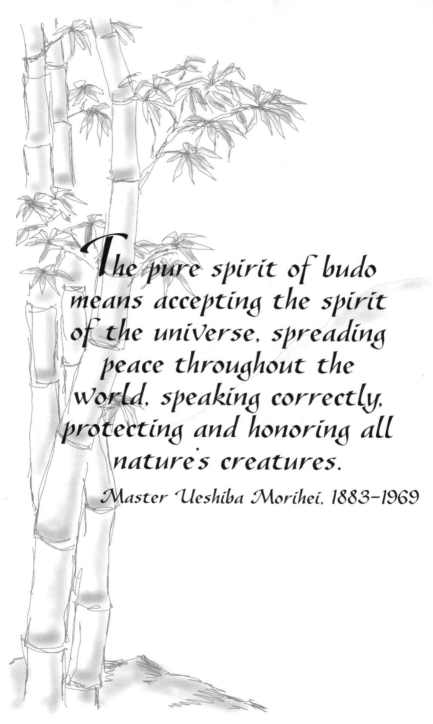

The pure spirit of budo means accepting the spirit of the universe, spreading peace throughout the world, speaking correctly, protecting and honoring all nature's creatures.

Master Ueshiba Morihei, 1883–1969

8
Share The Credit

If everyone in your *dojo* volunteers to clean up a park, let everyone enjoy the thank yous. If your karate demo team wins a competition or makes a good showing, be proud, step back and let everyone walk around with the trophy.

If your sales team meets its objectives or if your customer service department solves a tough problem, take everyone out to lunch. Let everyone laugh.

As a black belt or as a manager, your greatest satisfaction should come from seeing the people in your team, department or company succeed. Share the credit and experience the camaraderie. You know who you are. Let others glow in the feeling of accomplishing a mutual goal. Be enthusiastic for others. Acknowledge exceptional work. Encourage cooperation. Your reward will be employee loyalty.

The mountain rests on
the earth: the image
of splitting apart.
Thus those above
can insure their
position only by
giving generously to
those below.

I Chang, 1200 B.C.

9
Make Everyone Feel Important

Teach with enthusiasm and your love for your subject will spread. Sell your products or services with enthusiasm and your company will grow. Presume that your students and employees and customers are your equal because they are. Don't teach or sell down to anyone. Speak with and not at or to your students or customers. Learn and use peoples' names.

When you talk down to people, you shift the focus from your subject or product to your condescending attitude.

Make everyone you meet feel important. You can't be selectively likable. If you try to like some people and not others, you will eventually be seen as a phony and no one wants to do business with a phony. Those who don't appreciate your positive attitude will make their feelings known and you can move on to the majority who will welcome your efforts.

Look for opportunities to teach others about the Shaolin action principles. The principles may help them to find their own paths to personal fulfillment. Your reward will be many loyal friends.

A man should not associate with those who are greedy, clever talkers, flatterers or wasters. A man should associate with those who are helpful, willing to share happiness as well as sufferings, who give good advice and who have a sympathetic heart.

Buddha

10
Build Networks

You can go a long way by yourself, but you advance much better, much faster, with the help of others. Seek out others with a common purpose and help each other. Can the green belts meet for a special training session on Tuesday evening? Can all the business students who want to be entrepreneurs form a club and invite speakers?

Work through your mentors. Successful people in the martial arts and in business will not be threatened by your enthusiasm for success. Find them. Arrange to meet them. Tell them why you admire them. Then, sincerely ask for their help and often you will be warmly rewarded with positive suggestions and the names of contacts.

Form alliances for common purposes. Establish your own personal support systems. Where do you find good attorneys, accountants, physicians, investment advisors, dentists, tailors, mechanics or contractors? Ask those you respect for recommendations. Buy a contact management program for your computer, and as you meet new people add them to your personal network database. Form your support systems and personal networks before you need them. See Lesson #13 of the Winning With Small Business Course at www.success.org.

*Flow with whatever
may happen and let your
mind be free.
Stay centered by accepting
whatever you are doing.
This is the ultimate.*

Chuang-tzu, 369–286 B.C.

11
Think About Selling

You should be proud of your ability to make a good living for yourself and your family. If you make a good living, save, invest and retire early, you can devote your full time to your personal development and living in service to others.

If you offer a quality product or service that the market demands and you charge a fair price and you make your customers feel important, you will succeed.

One of the most lucrative business opportunities is commissioned sales. If you can sell, you'll never go hungry. However, selling is difficult for most people because a part of selling involves rejection. If there weren't a lot of rejection, companies wouldn't need salespeople. Unfortunately, most people take sales rejection personally. To succeed as a salesperson, you must believe in your product or service and its benefits enough that you welcome the opportunity to tell lots of people about them.

There are many commissioned sales opportunities: from real estate to insurance, from cars to cosmetics. Because selling is a tough job, there are opportunities to earn annual incomes well above average. Strive for nothing less.

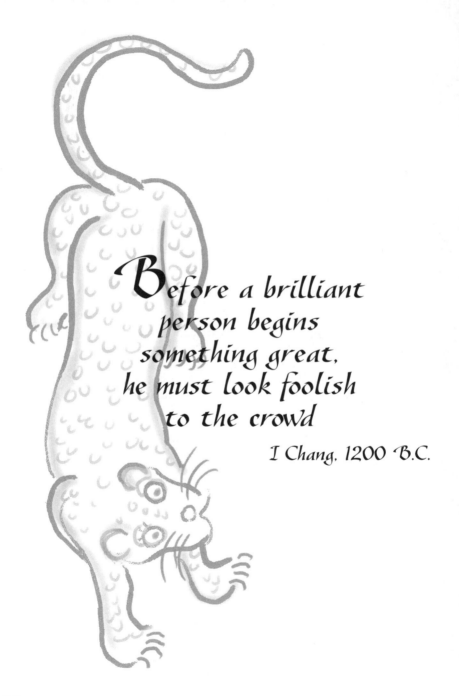

Before a brilliant person begins something great, he must look foolish to the crowd

I Chang, 1200 B.C.

12
Understand Courage

As a black belt, one may be called upon to be physically courageous but such events will be extraordinary. Even police officers and firemen and military personnel may only have to be physically courageous a few times in their careers.

Moral courage is needed more often than physical courage. Moral courage may mean the challenge to stay with a belief when your position may not be the most popular. Moral courage can be standing tall against bigotry, prejudice, unfairness and bullying behavior. Moral courage is a challenge to do what is right regardless of the personal consequences.

Think of people in physical pain or mental anguish. You may see courage being lived every day.

*Train with both heart
and soul without
worrying about theory.*

Gichin Funakoshi, 1869–1957,
Karate-Do, My Way Of Life

13
Stay Fit and Healthy

Be prepared to succeed both physically and mentally. You do not know when you will be called upon to defend with a block, a blow or a word.

If you want to be a versatile martial artist, you should cross train. You can swim, run, or rollerblade. Staying fit also helps to prevent injury and helps you deal with stress and fatigue.

If you want to be thinner, start putting out more calories than you take in and you will lose weight. Start now. If you want to be healthier, add more fruits and vegetables to your diet. Drink a lot of water. If you want a strong heart, do twenty minutes of vigorous forms or *katas* or calisthenics each day. If you want to look good and feel strong, work out with weights three times a week for thirty minutes. You don't need fancy gym equipment to be fit. You don't need a lot of time. You just need the will to start and persist. See Lesson #16 in the Winning With Small Business Course at www.success.org.

Man's life does not fill
a hundred years,

But always is full of
a thousand years' cares.

Short the midday,
bitter long the nights!

Why then do you not grasp
the lamp,

Seeking out for yourself the
short lived joys,

Why not today?

Why will you wait year
after year.

Ancient Chinese Poem

14
Write A Personal Mission Statement

Create for yourself an evolving document that outlines your purpose in life. Who are you? What are your values? What do you intend to do with your time to make your one life meaningful? Excepting acts of God, it is you who determines your future.

This book is now yours. Don't be afraid to underline sentiments and ideas you like and cross out those you don't. If you ruin the book and want another, don't worry, we'll sell you another copy. Your success is our mission. When you read inspirational passages in other books, magazines or newspapers, write them down or clip them out. Put everything together in a folder or box. This will serve as your motivational reserve and will help you create a personal mission statement.

Your mission statement only has to be a few sentences or paragraphs. Refer to your mission statement periodically and don't be afraid to change it as you grow.

A mission statement will help you to establish a foundation upon which you can build your dreams and goals and from which will flow your objectives and daily to-do list.

The superior man undergoes
three changes:

Looked at from a
distance, he appears stern.

When approached,
he is mild.

When he is heard to speak,
his language
is firm and decided.

Confucius, 551–479 B.C.

15
Be The Warrior

Be known as: youthful, successful, controlled, powerful, loyal, passionate, vital, noble, courteous, competent, confident, strong, polite, spiritual, cheerful, generous, honest, happy, kind, modest, centered, secure, disciplined, imaginative, capable, dynamic, motivating, calm, decent, fit, serene, romantic, charismatic, able, daring, diplomatic, patient, inspiring, courageous, vibrant, captivating, altruistic, cultured, clean, funny, enterprising, compassionate, brave, creative, prosperous, persistent, robust, charming, joyous, determined, sophisticated, respectful, hard working, humble, positive, active, thrifty, appealing, delightful, warm, chivalrous, considerate, frugal, unselfish, optimistic, affluent, peaceful, loving, diligent, curious, bold, tenacious, faithful, educated, principled, energetic and elegant. Establish your reputation. See BE THE MONK # 94.

*H*ave no friends not
equal to yourself.

Confucius, 551–479 B.C.

16
Build Your Team

In building your winning team for karate competitions or business success, don't be afraid to pick people who are stronger, faster, smarter, better organized, braver, more ambitious, funnier or more pleasant than you are. Ask your best people for recommendations. Always opt for quality.

You want your team to be built on excellence. You want your team built with members of merit and character. Resist those who propose membership based upon patronage, politics, quotas or diversity without reason. Excellence is excellence and is not subject to conditions of race, color, creed, national origin, etc. If someone is the best qualified person to fulfill the team's mission, then, that's what they are. If they are not, they are not.

People usually fail when they are on the verge of success. So give as much care to the end as to the beginning. Then there will be no failure. Keeping to the main road is easy, but people love to be sidetracked.

Lao-tzu, 600 B.C.,
The Way of Lao-tzu

17
Have Faith

Look around the train, the classroom or the office and you will probably see ordinary people who are going to live ordinary lives. There is nothing wrong with this choice. But you feel differently. You read this book and you feel empowered. You go to success.org for more training. Your mind fills with ideas. You find mentors. You research. You dare. You persist. You make money. You save. You invest. You succeed. You put your free time and extra money to good use.

Many around you could have done exactly the same thing. They didn't. You did. Why?

You can't easily answer this question. You must have faith. Thank God for making you extraordinary. Thank God for helping you see so many possibilities. Thank God for making you a person of action.

If the sage would guide the people, he must serve with humility. If he would lead them, he must follow behind.

Lao-tzu, 600 B.C.,
The Way of Lao-tzu

18
Ask Yourself

Are you generous enough to share your good fortune?

Are you healthy enough to keep to a regular exercise schedule?

Are you self-disciplined enough to stick to your prioritized to-do list?

Are you smart enough to be able to debate current affairs?

Are you brave enough to take a moral stand?

Are you self-confident enough to try new things?

Are you humble enough to ask to help?

Are you hard working enough to build your own business or professional career?

Are you strong enough to delay material gratification?

Are you merciful enough to forgive those who offend you?

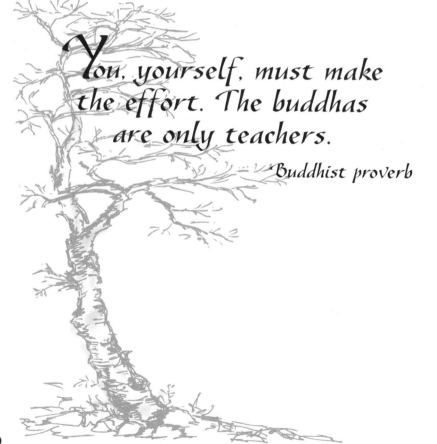

You, yourself, must make
the effort. The buddhas
are only teachers.

—Buddhist proverb

19
Seize The Moment

Be ready. There is no better time to start taking positive action than right now. You can't change yesterday but you can build today for tomorrow. You research and you seek advice while realizing that a time comes when you must act. Don't procrastinate.

One of the five Shaolin animals is the snake. The snake is supple and flexible. It is ready to adapt and seize opportunities. The snake strikes quickly to specifically targeted areas.

In the martial arts, there is a concept called *satori* which means to live in the moment. Do what you are doing now. Work now. Enjoy now. To the Shaolin monk, to know and to act were one and the same.

When you feel that you should change a bad habit, seize the moment and do it. When you feel like exercising, seize the moment and do it. When you feel like finally doing something that you have been putting off, seize the moment and do it. If you can help someone out, do it. If you can start practicing a new skill, do it. Fully participate in the present. Don't worry about the past or future. You are ready now.

Superior leaders get things done with very little motion. They impart instruction not through many words, but through a few deeds. They keep informed about everything but interfere hardly at all. They are catalysts, and though things would not get done as well if they weren't there, when they succeed they take no credit. And because they take no credit, credit never leaves them.

Lao-tzu, 600 B.C.,
The Way of Lao-tzu

20
Set The Example

Suppose you woke up tomorrow and you were the ideal you. Would you be: more daring, more powerful, more friendly, more accepting, more ambitious, more appealing, more giving?

In your mind's eye, see this new you. Start acting immediately as the person you will be, a person of character with a sound reputation. Your words, your manner, your attitude, your dress, your posture and your actions are all reflections. First you will see yourself as the new reflection and then others will begin to see the newly reflected you.

In modern society, people are constantly bombarded with visual and auditory messages. People need cues to sort good from bad and to find order so that they can make decisions. In many different aspects of your daily life, you are giving off cues which can be positive or negative. If you speak well, dress appropriately, smile, are courteous, have manners, work hard, volunteer and don't complain, you give people short cuts to view you in your best light. People will start to treat you as the new ideal you.

Be constantly on the lookout for heroes in your own life to admire and emulate. Adopt their styles. Then, lead by example. Find models to copy. Finish as the model.

We are what
we think.
All that we are
arises with our thoughts.
With our thoughts
we make the world.

Buddha

21
Act As If

If you feel happy, smile.

If you feel daring, act.

If you receive good service, compliment.

If you feel energetic, do something positive.

If you know a good joke, tell it.

If you feel generous, give.

If you are interested in getting wealthy, save and invest.

If someone needs help, lend them your strong hands
   or soft voice.

If you give your word, keep it.

If you can say something nice, say it.

If you can stand up for the weak, do it.

The secret of health for both mind and body is not to mourn for the past, not to worry about the future, but to live the present moment wisely and earnestly.

Buddha

22
Act Independently

Following the Shaolin, you are a person of action. You assess a situation and based on your knowledge and experience, you act. You dare. You risk. You make mistakes. You reevaluate. You act again. Your training has given you confidence. This is simple enough.

Because the status quo is often comfortable and safe, many people look for guarantees before taking independent action. They want assurances from others that all outcomes will be favorable. Yet, in seeking assurances, they frequently receive cautions. These cautions can easily be used as excuses for inaction. Those who love you the most may be the loudest in warning you not to risk failure.

If you always follow the crowd, you will always end up where the crowd ends up. You will never become a black belt if you think that you look foolish wearing a karate *gi*.

Make a personal decision to do what it will take to succeed. The Shaolin principles are known to many but lived by few. Most people know what they should be doing but lack either the will or the self-confidence to train for a black belt or start a business, or make an investment or establish a friendship. This is not the independent you.

A man's fortune must first be changed from within.

Chinese proverb

23
Seek Change

For there to be growth, there must be change. Since you seek growth, you must seek change. You must see yourself and your environment not only as it is but also as it could and should be. You seek the changes necessary to reach the better you so that you can play your small part in making a better world.

First, you change yourself.

Can you change your day and spend more time with your family? Can you change your standard lunch routine and take a walk? Can you change your drive home and stop at a nursing home for twenty minutes and visit someone who may have few visitors? Can you change your office habits and find the time to make five more phone calls? Can you change your customer service policies and handle more problems satisfactorily? Can you change your month and take one full day to visit and study your competitors?

What are the possible consequences of not changing?

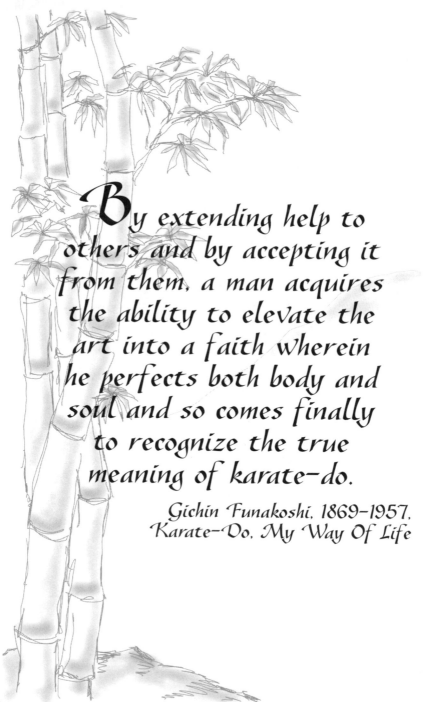

By extending help to others and by accepting it from them, a man acquires the ability to elevate the art into a faith wherein he perfects both body and soul and so comes finally to recognize the true meaning of karate-do.

Gichin Funakoshi, 1869–1957,
Karate-Do, My Way Of Life

24
Give Freely

The single best word in advertising is free. So give freely and reap the rewards.

If you are a hairdresser and need new customers, don't sit in the salon doing nothing. Hand out business cards, give free haircuts and show your expertise.

If you are a black belt, offer free self-defense clinics at factories, schools, fairs and anywhere else that will let you.

If you are an artist, donate one afternoon a month to teaching at the children's hospital.

Look for ways to say free and keep giving.

When you give with positive intent, you don't have to worry nor should you be worried about the benefits. You will feel good. You will feel appreciated.

There is a universal human law of reciprocity. When you give something to someone, that someone feels obligated to give something back. It could be new business. It could be media attention. It could be a testimonial letter. It could be a heart-felt *Thank you*.

Besides conditioning the body and improving speed, strength and coordination, karate increases one's alertness and self-awareness. It also teaches confidence — not cockiness or brashness but a deep confidence in one's abilities to deal with the world around him. And with confidence comes calmness and a sense of inner peace.

Mas Oyama, 1978,
Essential Karate

25
Communicate With Ease

Can you talk your way out of most tough situations? Can you talk your way through to decision makers to build up your sales? Can you talk to the media and garner positive press for your *dojo* or business? Can you talk to five hundred people and win converts to your cause or position? The answer to all is yes.

Being an effective communicator can take you a long way and is a Shaolin skill worth developing. Be yourself. It doesn't matter if you are talking to one person or one thousand. Be yourself. If you want people to like what you say, then persuade with modesty and build your audience up.

If you want to be good at karate, you practice. If you want to be good at public speaking, you practice. Practice one hour for each minute of your presentation or speech. Work on your pronunciation and vocabulary. Seek opportunities to speak in public. It's easy if you practice.

Listen to good communicators and model yourself after them. How do good interviewers ask questions? How do good public speakers speak? How do good salespeople sell? To communicate well, you can't get stuck on transmit. Pause before you speak. You must listen and speak with purpose.

Don't let technology leave you behind. Learn to communicate via e-mail and the Internet.

If you want to learn memorable phrases and ideas, see the Legendary Advice section at www.success.org.

The best time
to plant a tree
was 20 years ago.
The second best
is now.

Chinese proverb

26
Invest In Your Future

If you start training today, you may be sore tomorrow and a black belt in four years. If you buy a house today, you may have to work two jobs to make the mortgage payments now but you may own the house without debt in twenty years. If you give up TV tonight, you can take an evening course and in six years earn a college degree. Invest in yourself.

This is action. What are the consequences of inaction?

Most wealthy people save between 15% and 20% of their income. Invest in fields in which you have a specialized knowledge. If you sell cars, invest in the auto industry. If you are a real estate broker, buy income properties. If your hobby is antiques, buy antiques. Be sure to diversify your holdings by investing in a retirement plan and a no-load mutual fund.

Today, investors sacrifice and spenders enjoy. Tomorrow, investors enjoy and spenders keep working. There is a time value to money, so the earlier you start investing the better. Invest in things that appreciate rather than spend on things that depreciate. When you spend money, it is gone. When you invest money wisely, more money comes back. Without investment, there will be no return.

Most wealthy people own real estate and invest in stocks. For information on investing in real estate, a small business or the stock market go to www.success.org. It's all FREE.

When one treats people with benevolence, justice and righteousness and reposes confidence in them, the army will be united in mind and all will be happy to serve their leaders.

Chang Yu, 1000 A.D.

27
Appreciate Your Students

There is no need for black belts if there are no students. The black belt instructs students in karate so that the lessons to be learned from the martial arts can continue. You must encourage your students to be your ambassadors and bring in new students who in turn will bring in more new students.

Black belts must have students. Landlords must have tenants. Physicians must have patients. Accountants must have clients. Shopkeepers must have customers. Professional athletes must have fans. Writers must have readers. Employers must have employees.

It is people and only people who are going to give you their time or help or money, so that you can have everything that you ever wanted in your life for yourself and your family. It is only students and tenants and fans and customers and clients and patients. Appreciate them. They hold the keys to your success.

He who asks is a fool
for five minutes,
he who doesn't ask
remains a fool
forever.

Chinese proverb

28
Ask A Lot Of Questions

The best way for you to learn the martial arts is to ask a lot of questions of your master. Do not be shy. You want to be curious about a lot of new things. Questions are stepping stones to self-improvement. The only meaningless question is the question not asked. Dialogue will make you a better student.

As a *sensei*, a teacher, be open and not intimidating. Solicit questions and suggestions. Dialogue will make you a better *sensei*. Communicate with your master and students.

As a manager or business owner, you want to ask questions of your employees and customers. What do your employees need? Ask them often. What do your customers need? Ask them often. You need satisfied employees to satisfy your customers' needs and without satisfied customers, you are out of business.

Fast as the wind,
quiet as the forest,
aggressive as fire
and
immovable as
a mountain.

Samurai maxim

29
Run The Short Road

The short road leads you to a black belt. If you earnestly train three or four times a week, in three to four years you will probably earn your black belt. This is a short road to a notable accomplishment.

The short road leads to financial independence. If you offer a quality product or service and you appreciate your customer and you keep improving, you will earn enough money not to have to worry about it. This is a short road to a notable accomplishment.

The short road leads to strong personal relationships. If you smile at, listen to and are generous with family, employees and the public, you will be rewarded with many friends. If you are courteous, you will be welcomed anywhere. This is a short road to a notable accomplishment.

Waiting is not mere
empty hoping.
It has the inner certainty
of reaching the goal.

I Chang, 1200 B.C.

30
March The Long Road

Do not look at earning your black belt as a short-term sports accomplishment. On the long road, you must accept the responsibility of living your life as a Shaolin warrior-monk who is prepared to teach and share the way with others.

Just as earning a college degree is only the beginning of what should be a lifelong pursuit of knowledge, earning a black belt is only the beginning of a lifelong enjoyment of the martial arts.

On the long road you accept the responsibility of creating business success and being a good manager or employer and helping your employees reach their financial objectives. You should not view the amassing of material possessions as a singular measure of your success.

On the long road, experience beats inexperience, smart beats uninformed, effort beats laziness, polite beats rude, generous beats selfish, fit beats fat and interested beats bored. Be patient. Your time is coming. With time, everything passes from old hands to young.

On the long road, you accept the physical, mental and financial blessings that you will enjoy from following the Shaolin principles as you continue throughout your life to improve yourself and to give back to your family and society.

You are human.
You can improve,
and because you can
improve you can do
anything.

Confucius, 551–479 B.C.

31
Don't Always Apologize

As a black belt, your teaching will be well planned and organized. Your attitude will be giving. Your style will be strict but encouraging. This applies to most jobs.

You don't have to apologize if all of your students or employees don't work to their potential. This is their choice. Each student or employee will make an individual decision on whether to learn, to practice or work. Each will decide independently what the martial arts or a job can do for him or her. Or, with their own free will, they may decide to take a different road. You can encourage but you can't force your views on people who won't help themselves or look ahead. It is difficult to teach people who already know all of the answers.

Everyone who studies karate will not and should not reach black belt level. Everyone who starts a job won't become a manager. Doing your best as a teacher or supervisor is enough. You should not feel compelled to lower your standards to accommodate everyone.

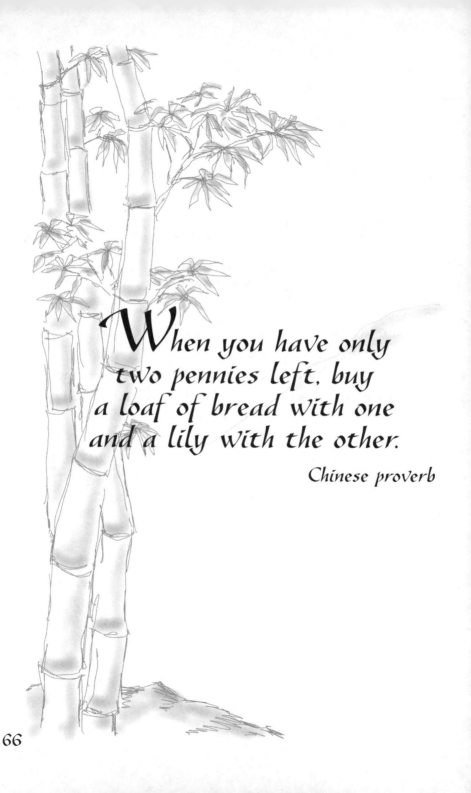

When you have only
two pennies left, buy
a loaf of bread with one
and a lily with the other.

Chinese proverb

32
Find Beauty Everywhere

You don't need a lot of money or time to lead a life filled with quality experiences.

You only need the will to check the cultural listings for local opportunities to see museum exhibits and regional theater companies and college symphonies.

You only need the energy to see sunrises and sunsets.

You only need the desire to take nature walks.

You only need the enterprise to go to free concerts or lectures.

You only need the ambition to live a full life. Appreciate all that your community offers. Take advantage. Vote to support the arts and be active in encouraging others to participate. If not you, who? If not now, when?

You can set the life enrichment process in motion by adding cultural activities to your to-do list.

Show me a man of violence who came to a good end and I will make him my teacher.

Lao-tzu, 600 B.C.,
The Way of Lao-tzu

33
Accept Differences

There is no single true way. To think that tae kwon do is better than Shaolin karate or that judo is superior to jiu jitsu, is wrong. Properly practiced, all of the martial arts have much to teach. There are true masters and fakers in all styles. Styles are not particularly important. There are martial artists and there are non-martial artists. Believe with confidence and trust that the vast majority of those who study and teach any of the martial arts do so with the right purpose and intention.

See each person as an individual and not as part of a group. All humans from all countries and cultures are equal without regard to race, color, creed or gender. Believe with confidence and trust that the vast majority of people whom you meet, befriend or do business with are more similar than different from you. Most people act in good faith. They mean you no harm and would assist you in time of need. Don't waste your time thinking otherwise.

Those who cannot
forgive others break the
bridge over which they
themselves must pass.

Confucius, 551–479 B.C.

34
Blame No One

Lying compromises your honor and making excuses compromises your strength. When you are wrong, the most expedient form of action is to admit your mistake and move on. Take the *buts* out of your life. Accept the fact that life isn't always fair.

You will not always be right. You are human and to err is human. Mistakes are your teachers.

By choosing to be a risk taker, you will face both peril and reward. You will make a lot of mistakes as all successful people have done and continue to do. It is not someone else's fault if your success involves persistence, failing and learning. Accept this as your choice. This is the nature of the road to success.

Let your ego go. Take responsibility. Worry more about what you can do rather than what others haven't done. Understand. Forgive quickly. Never feel sorry for yourself. Blaming others will not make you feel better. Try to see the other person's side.

If someone apologizes to you, be gracious, non-judgmental and move on.

In battle, combat is engaged directly with force, but victory is gained by surprise. Therefore the masters of the unpredictable are infinitely powerful, like heaven and earth, and inexhaustible as rivers. When they come to an end, they start again, like the cycle of days and months. When they die, they are reborn like the seasons.

Sun-tzu, 400 B.C.,
The Art of War

35

Be Outwardly Focused

People want to know where to find the best. Don't be shy or falsely modest. Tell them. It's you. You give karate lessons or sell insurance or mow lawns. Whatever you do, you try to do it well and you stand behind your product or service and you follow through and you say: *Thank you.* You constantly try to improve your business. People want the reassurance of hearing this. They will come to you and come back to you and you will succeed.

Ask all that you meet to buy your product or service. To help a lot of people, you must tell a lot of people what you can do for them. Hand out lots of business cards, write a newsletter, send e-mail, mail announcements, give speeches or hold seminars. Distribute a lot of the pocket-sized motivational books available from the American Success Institute. Not everyone will like or appreciate or be grateful to hear your message, but most will. In business, your fate lies not with the one prospect you are calling, but with the one hundred you are willing to call. Some will. Some won't. Move on.

You can be shy and work for fifty years. Or, you can believe in your product or service enough to be proud enough and brave enough to ask all to buy, and you may not have to work very long at all. The odds of succeeding when you deal with many prospects is high. The odds of succeeding when you are focused on the needs of others is overwhelming.

Don't hide. If you can't be proud of what you do or sell, then do or sell something else. You can't make people buy but you can let them know, if and when they are ready, that you will sell them a quality product at a fair price and that you will appreciate their business.

If a general and his men fear death and are apprehensive over possible defeat, then they will suffer defeat and death. But if they make up their minds from the general down to the last foot soldier, not to think of living but of standing in one place and facing death together, then though they have no other thought than meeting death, they will instead hold on to life and gain victory.

Yoshida Shoin, 1830–1859

74

36
Face Fear

Knowledge, practice and courage are your weapons against fear.

One person can step out of an airplane door at 2,000 feet without hesitation. Another can stand before an audience of 2,000 and give a speech without breaking into a sweat. Fears can be rational or irrational but they are always personal and real. Everyone fears something. Don't be afraid to be scared.

To diminish a fear, you must first face it. The one hundredth skydive or speech won't be as traumatic as the first. But you must make the first attempt. The best way to deal with first fears is through a combination of logic and bravery. Logically, most people who jump from planes or give speeches don't die. They succeed through preparation. If your equipment is right and your training is complete, you are ready to jump. If your speech is carefully crafted and you have practiced many times, you are ready to speak.

Associate with confident people. You have seen many who have already done what you fear doing. Now, do what they have done. Fear is learned and must be unlearned. After facing that fear, you will feel exhilarated. Without fear, there can be no courage. Fear provides the opportunity to be brave.

I do not know
whether I was
then a man dreaming
I was a butterfly,
or whether I am now
a butterfly dreaming
I am a man.

Chuang-tzu, 300 B.C.,
On Leveling All Things

37
Challenge Yourself

Don't look around at everybody else. If they play when they should be working, you don't have to. If they bake cakes when they should be exercising, you don't have to. If they need to belong to a certain group to find self-esteem, you don't have to.

If you follow the Shaolin way, you will be different. You will be a risk taker. You will be a hard worker. You will be a thinker. You will be a listener. You will be a helper. You will be a friend to those in need. You will meet objectives and set new objectives on your way to achieving your goals. You will adhere to a strict code of personal behavior.

This won't be easy. Few noble ideals are easy to attain. Meet the challenge. Step up. This will be you.

For inspiration, see the motivational quotes at www.success.org.

You cannot prevent
the birds of sorrow
from flying over your
head but you can
prevent them from
building nests in
your hair.

Chinese proverb

38
Follow Through

When sparring in the karate *dojo*, you have to pull your punches and kicks just short of actually hitting and injuring your opponent. You thereby develop the necessary but bad habit of hitting thin air. For sport and exercise this is fine but in self-defense near missing is losing. In self-defense, punches and kicks must be delivered not at the target but through the target. First, you penetrate your target with your mind and then follow through with your strike. To develop a feeling of full power follow through, you must practice your techniques on a heavy bag.

In business, follow through is very important. Finish the jobs you promise to finish. Follow through with your customer to ensure their satisfaction. Stay in touch with old students or customers. Let them know that you want them back. Ask for testimonials and referrals from satisfied customers and students. Ask satisfied customers for more business. It is easier to sell to an old customer than to find a new one.

Follow through on the heavy bag and be ready for real life encounters. Follow through in business and be ready for more. Follow through is an underutilized power tool in the martial arts and in business.

When you see a worthy person, endeavor to emulate him,

When you see an unworthy person, then examine your inner self!

Confucius, 551–479 B.C.

39
Choose Your Master First

While all karate styles offer benefits, all karate *dojos* are not created equal. Rather than looking for a style or *dojo*, your objective should be to find a karate master whose style and attitude suits yours. Since you will be devoting so much time and effort to your martial arts studies, you should research. Don't be intimidated or deterred. Sign up for a trial period and not a lifetime. Talk to students at different levels about their experiences. Find a *dojo* where the hours of operation and teaching schedules are compatible with your own.

If you want a good job, research the best companies to suit your needs. If you can, talk to the employees and to the managers before you apply. You should interview them because if they hire you, a Shaolin worker, they hire someone special.

If you want to start a business, do your research and work for the best people who are already in the business that you want to start. For you, every day at work will be a day at school. In a year or two, you'll be ready to soar.

If you are a student, do your research and find teachers who understand what you want to accomplish through your studies.

*If you want others
to be happy,
practice compassion.*

*If you want to be happy
yourself,
practice compassion.*

The 14th Dalai Lama

40
Do What You Love Doing

There are many martial arts styles from which to choose. Choose one that you love. Each of the arts properly practiced should lead you to a more productive and stress-free life.

There are 5,000 different types of occupations. Choose one that you love. People have been successful at all of them. They are your models. You can do the same. When you love your work, it doesn't seem like work. If you are caught in a dead end job, use your free time to find a job that you can love doing or start your own business.

There are unlimited activities to occupy your free time. Make sure that each of your days, weeks, months and years are full of activities that you love doing.

Plan to spend a lot of your time doing what you love. You are in control of your own happiness.

One moment of patience
may ward off great
disaster,

One moment of
impatience may ruin
a whole life.

Chinese proverb

41
How To Wear A Green Belt

You've arrived at the mid-point in your studies. You have proven yourself and been tested. Although a black belt is still several years away, you have shown the potential to earn one. Be encouraged.

Now, start acting differently. Volunteer to assist in teaching. Volunteer to vacuum the *dojo*. Volunteer to put up tournament posters. Start encouraging others to consider the multiple benefits gained through study of the martial arts.

In your own training, begin analyzing your movements and the reasons for them. What is the purpose of each move? What are the lessons to be learned from each form and combination? What is the consequence to each action? Now is the time to think. Shaolin is a thinking person's martial art.

In your business, keep focused on the bottom line through quality and customer service. Keep networking and looking for new opportunities.

It is worthy to
perform the present duty
well and without fail,
do not seek to avoid or
postpone it till tomorrow.
By acting now, one can
live a good day.

Buddha

42
How To Wear A Brown Belt

As a brown belt, you should be the worker bee of your karate *dojo*, ever in motion. While the green belt is encouraged to volunteer his or her efforts, the brown belt enjoys no such luxury. The brown belt is expected to act selflessly for the benefit of the karate *dojo*.

As a brown belt, you will have learned all the techniques you will ever need to be a complete martial artist. You will have learned a sufficient number of forms and combinations to be a highly skilled warrior. Now, you have to realize that you don't need to learn more but instead should keep practicing what you already know. The brown belt may think that he knows a lot but he may actually have little appreciation for the greater rewards of training that will come in the years ahead. Shaolin is a lifetime learning opportunity.

If you've started a business and it's running well or you have a comfortable job, don't just let the years pass unchallenged. Stay lean and hungry. Keep trying to learn and advance your career. There is a black belt level to working and that is to acquire sufficient assets that you don't have to work. You don't want to be comfortably working; you want to be comfortably retired.

Patience is power;
with time and patience
the mulberry leaf
becomes silk.

Chinese proverb

43
How To Wear A Black Belt

In the Shaolin style, to be a black belt is to be a teacher, coach and promoter.

To earn a black belt, as a teacher, you must demonstrate an understanding of your art to a sufficient degree that you can pass it along to your students. This ability to communicate is more important to the black belt concept than the endless personal accumulation of new techniques.

As a black belt coach, there is a responsibility to motivate your students. Everyone can improve with effort and practice if they make this choice. You will always be positive and encouraging.

As a black belt promoter, the martial arts need you to tell as many people as you can about the benefits that can be gained from study. You are a salesperson like other successful salespeople. How will people know the benefits of buying a particular car or house or landscaping service without being told by the salesman? To prosper in the next thousand years, the martial arts need your voice and example.

Without feelings of respect, what is there to distinguish men from beasts?

Confucius, 551–479 B.C.

44
Allow Your Opponent To Save Face

You won. That should be enough. Bragging is counterproductive. By boasting, you simply present the opportunity for your audience to think the opposite. It costs little for you to offer your opponent the opportunity to excuse his loss. In fact, you may gain appreciation from many observers.

To taunt or shame a defeated opponent may simply set the stage for another confrontation, with the odds stacked against you in the rematch. Your humiliated opponent may plot to redeem his lost honor by staging a rematch with more allies and more powerful weapons. You turn a quick battle into a long-term war. You set the stage for revenge and retaliation.

If you lose, do so with grace and good spirit. For you, there will be another day. If you win, be gracious in victory because some day very soon you will be vulnerable. Winning provides you with the opportunity to show both mercy and humility.

Learn as though you thought that you could never master it; hold it as though you would be in fear of losing it.

Confucius, 551–479 B.C.

45
Don't Be A Perfectionist

Trying to be perfect takes too much time and effort and creates too much stress and is impossible anyway. Instead, strive to relax at the 90% level. Following the Shaolin principles, reaching the 90% level in most of your financial and social endeavors will be something that you don't even have to think about because it will just happen through your persistence, determination, hard work and friendly personality.

Learn about the income and the lifestyle level of those in the top 10% of your profession. If you aren't content earning more than the 90% of your co-workers, choose another profession.

It is possible to try too hard in business, in exercise and in relationships. Overwork can produce stress and anxiety which is the opposite of the inner peace you seek. Your best is good enough. Live to a high standard and not to an impossible obsession.

I have three treasures.
Guard and keep them:
The first is deep love,
The second is frugality,
And the third is not
to dare to be ahead
of the world.
Because of deep love,
one is courageous.
Because of frugality,
one is generous.
Because of not daring to be
ahead of the world,
one becomes the leader
of the world.

Lao-tzu, 600 B.C.,
The Way of Lao-tzu

46
Applaud The Courage Of The White Belt

You walk into a karate *dojo* for a first visit and you see kicking and punching and blocking and chopping and flipping. It can be an intimidating atmosphere if you've never done these things before. You put on a white *gi* with a white belt and you may feel awkward and out of place. Yet, every black belt has done the same before you. This is your first day but there will never again have to be another first day, so persist.

All self-made businesspeople started small, made a lot of mistakes and built on the insights learned through hard work and continuing research. When they began, their ideas and goals may have seemed foolish and unrealistic, but they persisted.

Any new endeavor may be tough in the beginning. Accept this. You must believe in yourself. Some of your loudest critics may be those closest to you. When you ultimately succeed, everyone will claim to have been on your team from the beginning. Take action and persist. Applaud those who try, because the first step is often the toughest. Welcome the newcomer.

As the soft yield of
water cleaves
obstinate stone,

So to yield with life
solves the insolvable:

To yield, I have learned, is
to come back again.

Lao-tzu, 600 B.C.,
The Way of Lao-tzu

47
Read Biographies

What if you could learn the success secrets of the greatest people who ever lived? You can. The lives of the famous and the infamous have been duly recorded in biographies and autobiographies and are ready for you to read and research. You only have to take the action to go to the library or the book stores.

The lives of great martial artists, businesspeople and humanitarians are there. You will read about successes and triumphs. You will also learn how many times champions lose on their way to winning.

In reading biographies, you may come to the startling conclusion of how much greatness you possess. You may conclude: *Hey, I can do that.* You can decide to make your one life significant. Biographies help show you the way.

*Empty your cup so
that it may be filled;
become devoid
to gain totality.*

Bruce Lee, 1975,
Tao of Jeet Kune Do

48
Give Yourself The Gift Of Self-Reliance

If there is one gift that you can give yourself that will enhance the overall quality of your life, it is self-reliance. You already possess everything that you will ever need to succeed.

When you are self-reliant, if you lose your job, you'll get another. If you lose that job, you'll start your own business. You can make more money as a self-employed handyman applying the Shaolin action principles to your work than a lazy lawyer will ever earn. You need the will, the self-confidence and a realistic plan. As a follower of the Shaolin action principles, you will have them.

One of the five Shaolin animals is the tiger. The tiger is quick, strong and presumes victory. He knows no other way. He doesn't try to impress. There is no need.

Life just can't seem to get you down because you are too much in control of yourself.

*Great souls have wills,
feeble ones
have only wishes.*

Chinese proverb

49
Focus On Your Priorities

You could be doing a million things but you should pick one. What is the one most important thing that you want to do today, this week or this year? You should be able to answer this question quickly. This action principle is a common denominator among the successful. They are focused on the immediate accomplishment of specific objectives.

If you don't prioritize your day's activities, everything is of equal importance and nothing is of singular importance. Whether one thing gets done or doesn't get done, may not matter. You want your activities to be important. You want to feel the pleasant sense of accomplishment often.

In the martial arts, there is *kime* which means to tighten the mind, focus, and to exclude all extraneous thoughts that are not essential to the immediate objective at hand.

Write your to-do list every day. Prioritize it. Keep to the first item until it is done. Feel good. Move to item two. Feel good. Put first things first.

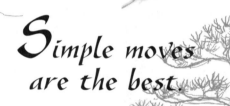

*Simple moves
are the best.*

*Bruce Lee, 1975,
Tao of Jeet Kune Do*

50
Don't Complicate Matters

In the martial arts, there is the concept of *shibumi* which means to pare away the unnecessary so that you can get to the necessary. Don't complicate your life. Look for the simple ways or answers first.

For opportunity, you only have to open your eyes and ears and listen to your heart.

For money, you can start a business tomorrow based on the Winning With Small Business Course at www.success.org.

For physical security, you can become a black belt.

For financial independence, you can invest your savings.

For love, find a spouse.

For education, you can go to the libraries and bookstores tomorrow and teach yourself.

For generosity, give to charity.

For organization, give away everything that you haven't worn or used in a year.

For friends, bless them with your kindness.

Pare away the unnecessary. You don't have to listen to those who may be saying that you are too old, too young, too weak, too poor, too unattractive, too uneducated or the wrong color, gender or nationality. They are not speaking of someone following the Shaolin principles.

*If you can, help others;
if you cannot do that,
at least do not
harm them.*

Dalai Lama

51
Assume Leadership

As a follower of the Shaolin principles, you are the exception. You are willing to work harder and be more generous than you have to be. You will exhibit character, vision, passion, enthusiasm and patience. You will be ready to inspire and lead.

You will accept responsibility. You will maintain the highest standards as you set the rules. You will be consistent. You will have a clear vision of your mission. You will encourage teamwork and the formation of strong alliances.

You will set the example. You operate at the black belt level. In dress, speech, demeanor and attitude, you show the way to your students. Your values and ideals have been deeply considered. You guide yourself and others toward excellence, not perfection. You are always open to new ideas, suggestions and offers of assistance. You must never ask or expect others to do what you would not do.

You will believe in your students and employees and they will reward you with their support.

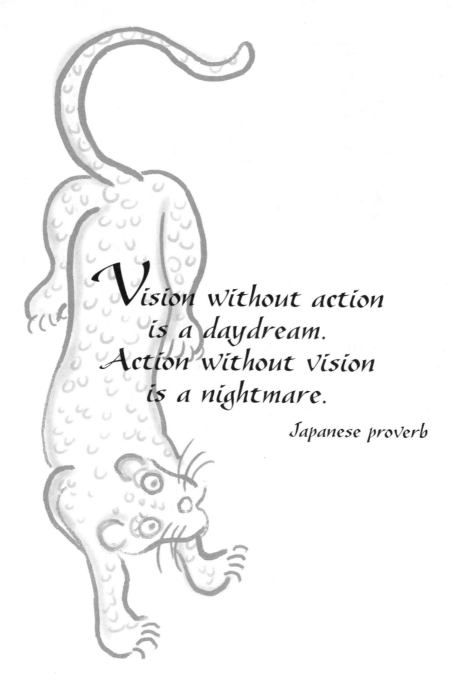

*V*ision without action
is a daydream.
Action without vision
is a nightmare.

Japanese proverb

52
Listen To Your Instincts

I don't feel comfortable here. I don't like the sound of this. This doesn't look right to me.

Whether with regard to your physical self or your physical surroundings, your intuition and instincts are your own best early warning system. Listen to the inner voice. Listen to that gut feeling. Go to the doctor. Leave the party and go home. Take a taxi home. Get away from these people. Quit this job.

Every once in a while, your instincts may be off and you may feel foolish. Err on the side of safety and your instincts may be saving you from danger. Give yourself time or space to consider your options. It would be foolhardy to do otherwise.

The same is true in business. If you feel that you have a good idea, try it. If you feel that you've made a mistake, correct it and move on.

*If you want to do your
duty properly,
you should do just
a little more than that.*

Bruce Lee, 1973

53
Accept Hard Work

Your interest in learning will never wane. Your willingness to do for others will never disappear. Your commitment to high personal standards will not cease. Your dedication to the martial arts won't stop. Commit yourself to hard work and be thankful that you aren't lazy. Laziness makes all work difficult. Great accomplishments come from hard work. Luck accompanies hard work.

If necessary, be prepared to endure temporary hardship. It won't always be easy. Most people who start karate could become black belts but few do. Most people who start their own businesses could become wealthy but few do. Most people could give more time and money to worthwhile social causes but few do. At times, the work is going to be hard to do and you would prefer doing something easier. Accept this.

From day one, you accept the premise that in following the Shaolin way, you will have to work hard and give much. Don't cheat or look for the easy way out. Bask in the feeling of exhilaration of accomplishment that few will experience. If you are willing to work hard, you will never go hungry. In the end, you will be very happy to discover that all the hard work was worth it.

One of the most striking features of karate is that it may be engaged in by anybody, young or old, strong or weak, male or female.

Gichin Funakoshi, 1869–1957,
Karate–Do, My Way Of Life

54
Remain Flexible

Many martial arts class begin with stretching to improve flexibility and loosen the muscles and joints for the rigorous workout to follow. Flexibility may help prevent physical injury.

In a match, a skilled martial artist is patient and flexible. He or she is open and without expectations. He or she is ready to switch from one technique to another.

In daily life, through a love of many things, it is also possible to remain flexible. If it starts raining on the way to the beach, you'll enjoy going to the movies. If you are kept waiting for an appointment, you won't get angry but instead make a few calls or work on your schedule. If you get stuck in traffic, you'll enjoy your favorite motivational audio tape, your favorite radio station or CD.

The small stuff just can't get you down.

In the midst of great joy do not promise anyone anything. In the midst of great anger do not answer anyone's letter.

Chinese proverb

55
Play To The Winners

You have one life to live. You want to be happy and to make your life meaningful. You haven't got time to waste time associating with negative people. They will drain your energy and when they find a willing or captive audience, they won't let it go. Negative people may have justifiable concerns but too often they get over involved in minor matters and imaginary transgressions. Negative people may be envious of your ability to succeed. They may feel guilty knowing that they aren't willing to pay the price that success asks.

Negative people are usually negative because they have ceded control of their happiness to others, often many others. It's the boss, the neighbors, the kids, the politicians, the police. It's money. It's the bills.

Be polite and encouraging to negative people. Listen to their complaints or stories but only once. Give them a copy of this book. It may help. If their problems are serious enough, guide them to professional help. Don't judge. Empathize with them but avoid being drawn into their web of unhappiness. Help those you can while realizing that you can't help or save everyone. You can open your heart, be compassionate and still be strong enough to walk away. You can say no. Everyone has problems but not everyone allows those problems to rule them. You can offer a temporary safe haven without becoming a permanent home. You do not have to sacrifice your life to the problems of another.

He who is really kind,
can never be unhappy;

He who is really wise,
can never be confused;

He who is really brave, is
never afraid.

Confucius, 551–479 B.C.

56
Be Open To New Ideas

Your *sensei* (martial arts teacher), your customers, your employees, your family, your friends, your suppliers and even your competitors may all have suggestions that you can put to profitable use.

Find new ideas in books, magazines, videos, audio tapes, newsletters, trade literature and on the Internet. Find new ideas at conventions, seminars, lectures and by taking evening courses. Find new ideas by networking at the Chamber of Commerce and at other professional and civic organizations.

Be open to the fact that lots of people are going to have ideas worthy of your consideration. Welcome them. Incorporate the better ideas into your training and business.

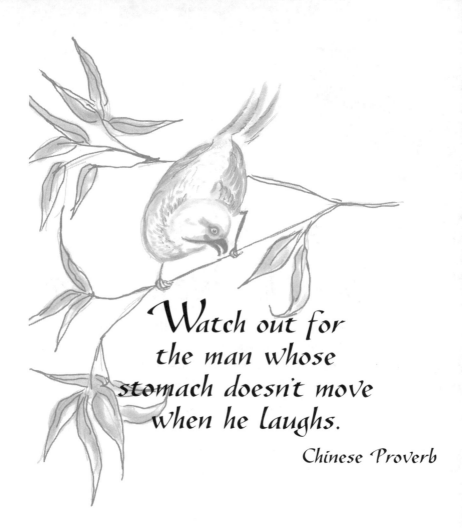

Watch out for
the man whose
stomach doesn't move
when he laughs.

Chinese Proverb

57
Heed The Warnings

High voltage. Wear Your Seat Belt. Capacity Limited to 150. Danger - Thin Ice. Don't Drive Drunk.

You may wish that you were invulnerable but you are not. You are human and your human body can get easily hurt if you aren't a vigilant guardian of your own physical safety. Awful accidents may happen beyond your control. They are accidents and acts of God. But we are also often forewarned. A prudent warrior appreciates the warnings.

On occasion, you will find yourself in the company of stupid people who don't care about their own safety or yours. Be courageous. Speak up and then leave them to their stupidity.

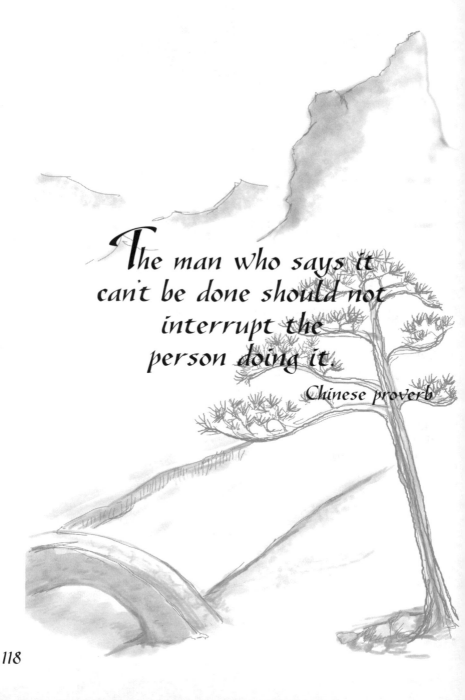

The man who says it can't be done should not interrupt the person doing it.

Chinese proverb

58
Set The Bar High

Measure yourself against the best. Most others will choose to be average. This is what average means. You can choose to say: *Yes, this may be so but this is not me!* You won't know where your limits are if you don't keep trying. Reject the idea of good enough. Commit to excellence.

As a teacher or a businessperson, you may have to accept mediocre performance from your students and employees but you do not have to take the easy path and reward it. Set the bar high for those in your charge. They will be the better for it.

When you continue to challenge yourself, you will find that few goals are beyond your grasp. Set standards that give your students the opportunity to show their capabilities and spirit.

Learning is a treasure that will follow its owner everywhere.

Chinese proverb

59
Practice Your Katas

Katas are a series of formalized moves in which you confront imaginary opponents. Congratulations; you defeat them every time. Repetition builds muscle memory, preparing you to react instinctively if an actual need arises. *Katas* show you how to react. *Katas* approach perfect practice. In a *kata*, every move is important. To be more than just a dance, *katas* must contain your spirit. You must concentrate.

In school, you must fill your studies with your spirit. What is the purpose of each course that you are taking? Each course should mean more to you than simply being a part of someone else's curriculum. You will study hard. Know why.

In business, your spirited commitment to a consistent pattern of quality and service will bring you a stream of loyal customers. Your customers will expect the best and you will deliver no less.

The Way of Heaven has
no favorites.

It is always with
the good man.

Lao-tzu, 600 B.C.,
The Way of Lao-tzu

60
Define Integrity

As a follower of the Shaolin way, you are: proud, strong, friendly, generous and successful. Many will seek your counsel. Others will have an envious eye on you, just waiting to find fault. Being human, you will probably not disappoint either group.

Have faith and a belief in your cause. Know what you will fight for and what you won't. Do not compromise what is right.

Make your word your bond. Keep your promises. Fulfill your commitments. People want to know where you stand and for what you stand. People respect honesty and sincerity. People hate hypocrisy.

Deliver what you promise. You cannot speak stronger words than: *I give you my word.*

The Master always
teaches without
teaching.

Tao Te Ching, 72

61
Follow Your Code of Honor

As a follower of the Shaolin action principles, you choose to adhere to a strict code of honor regarding your personal behavior.

You do not need to prove your might at the expense of others.

You do not need diplomas, awards or the acclaim of others to know who you are.

You do not need an audience to do the right thing.

You do not need a lot of money or many physical possessions to be happy.

You do not need to stand first in line.

You do not need lessons to act civilly.

You do not need prompting to help someone in need.

My true religion
is kindness.

14th Dalai Lama

62 Stay Centered

Stand with your knees slightly bent. Head up. Breathe deeply from your belly. You are a very small part of the grand scheme of things. You are one with the universe. You are everything and nothing. Remain calm, balanced and aware.

Take pride in your studies and your work. In the battles of life, you will take punches. Some may hurt. This too will pass. Yet, as you stay close to the Shaolin way of hard work and generosity you will be drawn ever closer to a destiny of fulfillment.

You are the center of your universe. Take care of your own needs first. Then, go to your family. Then, go to your friends and employees. Then, move on to the larger communities. Don't use saving the world as an excuse to forget your family.

The power of commitment
is wondrous and can
transcend all other forces.

Shihan Tak Kubota, 1977,
The Art of Karate

63

Commit To Self-Discipline

If becoming a financial success were easy, everyone would do it. It isn't. They don't. As a follower of the Shaolin action principles, you can.

You can keep your word even though with hindsight this may not always be easy. You can write and focus on your goals and objectives and your to-do list. You can exercise your body when you're tired. You can read business materials. You can volunteer. You can give a little extra money to charity. You can give a little extra time to family members, students and customers. You can pick up litter on the jogging path. You can delay gratification. You can do a lot while others are idle.

You won't always want to do these things. You will feel that you are doing more than your share. You are right. Work on it. You are tough.

A bird can roost but on
one branch.

A mouse can drink
no more than its fill from
a river.

Chinese proverb

64
Accept Your Limitations

You can't do everything and some things you can do better than others. If you can punch better than you can kick, you emphasize your punches. As you face your opponent, pause and reflect. There are many ways to find victory. Rely on your strengths. To know your strengths, you must first acknowledge and then compensate for your weaknesses. Some will never be able to execute a high kick with power. So, they learn leg sweeps and accomplish the same objective.

Ask your friends and mentors: *What am I good at?* Don't be afraid to ask for advice or help and don't be afraid to listen to the answers. Reflect and learn.

Shaolin karate is an eclectic martial art which encourages experimentation and adaptation at the black belt level.

In business, solicit comments on your products and services. Customer and employee compliments and complaints are important tools to improve efficiency. Who knows you better?

Accept your limitations. Accept your circumstances. Do your best being who you are with the abilities you have. Following the Shaolin action principles, you should have more than enough of everything to succeed.

A bit of fragrance
always clings to
the hand that gives
you roses.

Chinese proverb

65
Be Grateful To Your Sensei

We all have *senseis* to thank. They are our teachers.

Learning is a process of self-discovery. Usually, that self-discovery is based on the trial and error and experience of those who have come before us. Someone ventured forth from the safe warmth of the prehistoric camp fire. Someone hankered for a better life overseas. The curiosity and bravery of others has given us the knowledge to live long, comfortable lives. The human race is stronger and more adaptable today than ever before.

Be grateful for the explorers and scientists. Be grateful for soldiers who won our freedom. Be grateful for the politicians who protect our freedom. Be grateful for the *senseis* who pass the martial arts traditions on to us. Be grateful for all teachers who pass the love and enthusiasm for their subjects to us.

Continue down the path. Respect those who work on your behalf. Respect comes from being respectful. Some day, you will be old and you will appreciate the repayment of others' kindness. After class, thank the *sensei*.

*Life unfolds on
a sheet called time
and once finished
is gone forever.*

Chinese proverb

66
Retire Early

If you didn't have to worry about earning a living, you could concentrate on your Shaolin monk's work of developing your personal potential and being in service to others.

You don't have to be a millionaire to retire early. In fact, if you had savings of half that amount, which you invested prudently, you could retire and earn an annual income that exceeds the annual income of 75% of the people in the United States.

Over half of the people in the United States have less than $10,000 saved for retirement and live from paycheck to paycheck. They have no definitive financial plans. You are different. You now have a financial goal to retire early.

Consider this: After 20 years of saving 20% of your income, you may create the choice of not having to work for a living.

Consider this: As an alternative to saving 20%, can you earn 20% more if you work 10 hours a day rather than 8, or 6 days a week rather than 5?

*Be extremely subtle,
even to the point of
formlessness.
Be extremely
mysterious, even to the
point of soundlessness.
Thereby you can
be the director of the
opponent's fate.*

Sun–tzu, 400 B.C.,
The Art of War

67
Observe And Be Aware

At first observation and awareness will require conscious effort on your part. Over time, it will become instinctive and will prove to be one of your most valuable skills.

In self-defense, you enter a movie theater and you make a mental note of the exits. You walk down an unfamiliar street and automatically scan for the unusual.

In business, you see ads and get ideas for your ads. You shop in stores and get ideas for your store.

Personally, you see how the fashionable are dressed. You dress conservatively and appropriately for the occasion.

Listen to the speech patterns of powerful people. Be silent. Think twice and speak once. Be an active listener. Look at the person who is talking. Don't interrupt. Ask questions. Be aware of their body language. Listen and they will like you. Your self-confidence in mind and body will create a charismatic aura.

Be alert. Life isn't a blank stare. Stay informed. Read newspapers, magazines and books. Watch the news. See what is around you, learn and adjust.

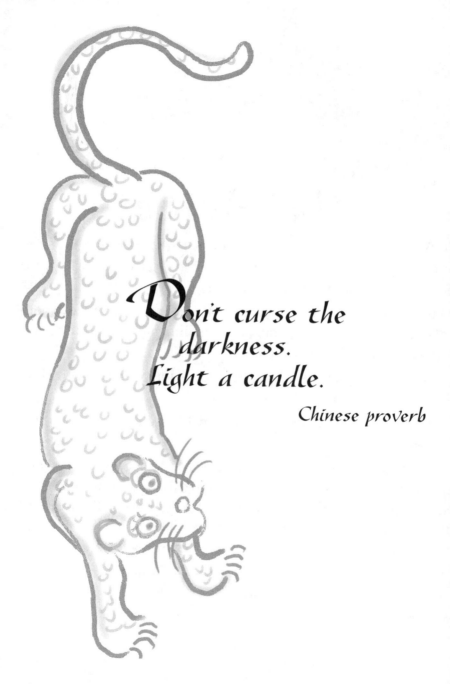

Don't curse the
darkness.
Light a candle.

Chinese proverb

68
Go Ahead

You don't have to wait for permission to do the right thing. Do it now. If you can't go to the karate *dojo* for ninety minutes, go for forty minutes. If you don't have time to send a letter to a sick friend, send a card, a fax or an e-mail. If you can't visit your mother, call her. If you see a gift that a friend would love, buy it for him or her.

Many times you will find excuses for not doing things because you can't get everything done exactly the way you'd originally planned. Yet, be bold and get in the habit of doing something. Walk down one block. Pay three bills. Take fifteen minutes with your children's homework. Give five dollars to charity. Small efforts done continually can yield significant, positive results. Do it now while it's on your mind.

You don't have to be perfect to live the Shaolin way. Just be a person of action. You must have more than good intentions to succeed. You must act. Go ahead.

Loyalty, a spirit of justice and bravery are the three natural virtues of the samurai.

Daidoji Yuzan, 1639–1730, Budo Shoshin Shu

69
Love Many Things

You proportionally increase your chances for happiness by increasing the number of things that you love doing. Love many things and your happiness will escalate into an enthusiasm for life which will have a positive effect on you and those around you.

To love many things, you must be adventurous enough to try new things. Be excited and passionate about life. Feel good. You must be able to see beauty in the grand scheme of things as well as in details.

Discover: karate, theater, music, art, books, food, yoga, wine, sports, travel, dance, movies, sunsets, solitude, beaches, exercise, friends, gardens, Tai Chi, fashion and the Internet. Open your mind. Find your personal preferences. Make your home, office and *dojo*, beautiful places to love. Keep going …

Remember how lucky you are to have so many interests. Happiness may not be a result of financial success. Happiness is a result of loving many things.

*Govern a great nation as
you would cook a small
fish. Do not overdo it.*

Lao-tzu, 600 B.C.,
The Way of Lao-tzu

70
Live Simply

You work hard and you and your family deserve to enjoy the fruits of your efforts. Don't be ashamed of your accomplishments. You should have nice things; you just don't need everything. When you want everything, you sentence yourself to a life of toil without respite. You want to work for what you need. You do not have to sentence yourself to hard labor for the false trappings of status. Be pragmatic.

Live below your means. Prepare and follow a sensible budget with dollars for investment as a top line item. Think not only about earning more but also about spending less. Pay off your credit cards. Can you cut your expenses by 10% - 15%? Can you be frugal and delay some material gratification and invest the savings?

If you follow the Shaolin action principles during your asset building years, an economic miracle may happen for you. As others must work forty or fifty years before retirement, you may only have to work half as long on the money-centered part of your life.

Living on less can eventually yield you much more. The simpler you make your life, the easier it will be to find and maintain success. Think in terms of moderation. You can make a comfortable life for yourself by finding contentment in the things you already have and holding reasonable expectations.

*O*ne kind word can warm
three winter months.

Japanese proverb

71
Make Today Special

Take the sameness out of your days. Give each day a specific purpose. What do you want to accomplish at work that will bring you one day closer to your financial goals? How do you intend to keep yourself healthy? What fun things can you look forward to doing today? How can you make someone else's day better than it might be?

For unsuccessful and unhappy people, there is often a boring sameness to their days. Is it Monday or Thursday? It doesn't matter. Is it March or November? It doesn't matter. Is it 3 o'clock in the afternoon or 10 o'clock in the morning? It doesn't matter.

Everybody has the same amount of time each day. How are you going to spend your 24 hours today? Plan your days in advance. Make lists. Lists are your personal road map to personal accomplishment and balanced living. Always carry paper and pen with you. What are you doing today to ensure a better tomorrow for yourself and your family?

Those who realize their folly are not true fools.

Chuang-tzu, 300 B.C., On Leveling All Things

72
Record Your Thoughts

Carry index cards, tap on a hand-held computer, carry a small notebook or borrow napkins to write on. As you become an action-oriented person, positive thoughts will occur with increasing regularity. Write down your ideas. You will have good ideas because you will have many ideas. Review your notes before your quiet time or before bed. You will become your own best therapist. You will see the ways to solving your own problems, finding your own route to happiness and realizing your own dreams. Spend most of your time thinking about solutions and not problems. Get back to recording your thoughts.

Manifest plainness,
Embrace simplicity,
Reduce selfishness,
Have few desires.

Lao-tzu, 600 B.C.,
The Way of Lao-tzu

73
Be Of No Mind

At the decisive moment in combat, the warrior acts. The repercussions of the action must be borne by the generals and politicians. The warrior simply acts without thought based on his training and mandate. In the martial arts, this is called *mushin*.

In combat, the warrior cannot be concerned with loss or injury because to harbor such thoughts simply creates an opening that the enemy can exploit. To be successful, the warrior relies upon his instincts developed through his training as if with no mind. The combat experience reflects back the spirit you put into your karate practice. It mirrors the dedication. The time for thought was during meditation and reflection.

In business, you may be able to solve a customer service problem faster by just picking up the phone, acceding to the customer's request and moving on, rather than trying to think up ways to win against the customer. From following the Shaolin principles you will form positive habits. These habits will allow you do the right things without thinking. You will be acting quickly and prudently in your own long-term interest.

*Nobody can take away
my strength since I do not
use it. The best technique
is to avoid combat.*

Master Ueshiba Morihei, 1883–1969

74
Forget Everybody

Not everybody wants to do business with you. Not everybody wants to be your friend. Not everybody is going to be nice to you. Not everybody wants world peace. Not everybody wants to work hard. Not everybody wants to be president.

Not everybody is smart enough to be a rocket scientist. Not everybody is fast enough to run in the Olympics. Who is helped by pretending otherwise?

Trying to accommodate everybody is a trap. It can't be done. Be yourself. Not everybody will listen to reason or even act in his or her own best interest. Most do. You can.

Softness triumphs over hardness, feebleness over strength. What is more malleable is always superior over that which is immoveable. This is the principle of controlling things by going along with them, of mastery through adaptation.

Lao-tzu, 600 B.C.,
The Way of Lao-tzu

75
Maintain Your Sai

In the martial arts, your *sai* is your presence. Let your *sai* speak for you. Your *sai* flows out from within. Have confidence from your training. You can get the job done.

Your contented presence shows an air of simple elegance and refinement in your attitude and form. You appear physically, emotionally and spiritually strong and yet you seem to have even greater strength stored in reserve. You are poised, coordinated and balanced. You command with effortless confidence. Be calm. Be deliberate. Feel assured and alert. Look good. Feel good. Keep your head up and your shoulders back. Keep your eyes forward. Breathe deeply. Walk with a purpose. Have a firm handshake. Your eyes are friendly. Let your smile begin in your mind. You exhibit both style and class.

You breathe low and deep from your *tantian* which is a point just three fingers below your navel. Breathe with steady short inhales and longer exhales. This is where your *chi,* your energy, resides.

The odds are with you. You are part of a Shaolin tradition that has survived for hundreds of years. You are the product of millions of years of human evolution. You have a family heritage and a nationality of which to be proud. Take pride in who you are and in those values and beliefs for which you stand. Bask in the feeling of being your best.

The things you want drawn to you will come as a result of your good nature and determined persistence. Pause and savor the moment. Begin your work. You have already intimidated your opponents and charmed your followers.

He is poor who does not feel content.

Japanese proverb

76
Count The Time

How long does it take to practice your *katas*?

How long does it take to stay informed?

How long does it take to be well groomed?

How long does it take to read your child a bedtime story?

How long does it take to say a kind word or deliver a compliment?

How long does it take to clean up after a meal at a shelter?

How long does it take to complete the next entry on your to-do list?

Probably just minutes.

He who is contented
is rich.

Lao-tzu, 600 B.C.,
The Way of Lao-tzu

77 Imagine

Imagine that you can give your family all the money they need.

Imagine that you can give your family all the time with you they need.

Imagine that you will be seen as a respected leader in your community.

Imagine that your students will like you.

Imagine that your employees will work hard for you.

Imagine that people are telling you that you are making a difference in their lives.

Imagine that you can accomplish all that you want to accomplish by yourself.

This is not a daydream. This is Shaolin.

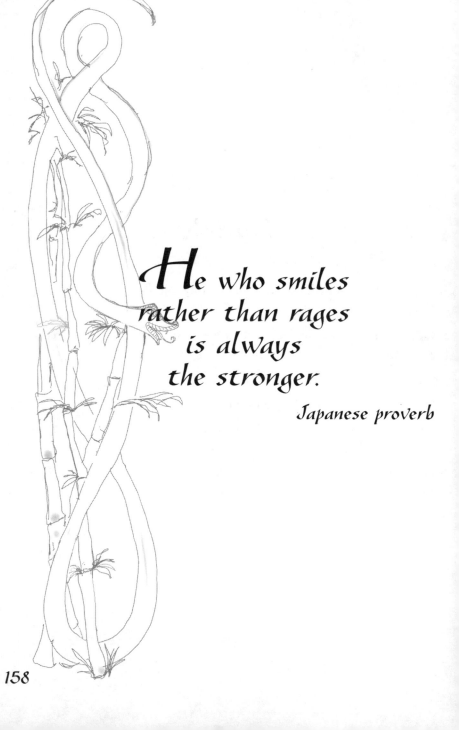

He who smiles
rather than rages
is always
the stronger.

Japanese proverb

78
Walk Away

Nobody who dares to challenge the status quo wins them all.

Be prudent. Take a deep breath and think. Perhaps the smartest course of action is to retreat and reflect upon your options. Just because you are in the right and deserve victory doesn't mean that you will, in fact, win every fight, every game or every argument. Someone else may have the tactical advantage. Maybe you can go around them. Maybe you can regroup your resources for a counterattack. Maybe you can seek allies. Maybe the spoils of victory aren't worth the effort or risk. Fallen heroes are often quickly forgotten.

One of the five Shaolin animals is the crane. The crane is agile and yielding. The crane redirects and persists, allowing an opponent to defeat itself with its own momentum. It is smart enough to retreat when outmatched.

Have the self-confidence to know when not to fight. You don't always have to be right.

*Fool me once
shame on you.
Fool me twice
shame on me.*

Chinese proverb

79
Work at Work

Work expands to fill the time available. Many people will work only up to expectations. Some work just hard enough to not get fired. Some people actually work as little as half the time that they are at work. These people create a window of opportunity for you succeed. Don't worry about being obligated to work more hours to beat the competition. You probably don't have to invest more time. Instead, if you commit to working all the time that you are at work, you will probably come out well ahead of your competition.

However, don't become lulled into mistaking activity for accomplishment. Follow your prioritized to-do list. Live and appreciate every day as an important day.

Seek not happiness too greedily, and be not fearful of unhappiness.

Lao-tzu, 600 B.C.,
The Way of Lao-tzu

80
Inch Forward

Modern life can make you soft both physically and mentally. You can be lulled into mediocrity very easily. The status quo may become comfortably familiar. You can actually begin to believe that you are doing all that you can do or that doing more isn't worth the effort.

In the martial arts, there is the concept of *kaizen* which means a dedication to continual improvement. Challenge yourself. You must start the positive momentum in your life.

You don't need someone else to tell you not to smoke. If today, you smoked a pack, tomorrow smoke 18. The next day, 17. Improve. If you haven't read a book recently, read one. If you don't exercise, take a walk around the block. If you can swim 30 laps, swim a mile. If you're shy, say to five new people: *Good morning!*

You know yourself. You know what self-improvement you need. You don't need anyone to tell you not to jump from a fifty-story building, so why would you need someone to tell you not to do drugs, to exercise more, to eat a sensible diet, to talk to your kids, or to compliment your employees? You know what to do.

Be strong. Take that step. Do the hard thing. Challenge the you who is content with yesterday's accomplishments. Take a deep breath. The tortoise often beats the hare. Improve incrementally. Changes that last a lifetime begin moment by moment.

H e who knows
does not speak.

H e who speaks
does not know.

Lao-tzu, 600 B.C.,
The Way of Lao-tzu

81
Stop Talking

Resolve to be constructive. Resolve to be a part of the solution.

It is easy to stand on the side of the mat, not participate and find fault. It is easy not to volunteer. It is easy to talk of good works while leaving the real work to others. As a follower of the Shaolin way, you must do more than talk. You must be a person of action.

Whom do you think really wants to listen to your problems?

You do not have to change the world. Small recurring involvements are fine. Your small everyday actions can set a quiet example for others to follow. Befriend the unfortunate who has no friends. Ask him how he's doing. Listen to the answer. Time required: 2 minutes. Pick up the discarded paper on the public street. Time required: 6 seconds. Attitude. Example. Discipline. Shaolin.

A closed mind is like
a closed book, just a block
of wood.

Chinese proverb

82
Look Forward To Tomorrow

You can begin immediately to be the person that you aspire to be. You don't have to wait. You do not have to be ruled by yesterday. In fact, change is often easy. The hard part is to maintain that change for the long term.

Hope does spring eternal. If you fall down today, you have tomorrow. If you fall down tomorrow, you still have the day after tomorrow. Keep at it.

The leopard is one of the five Shaolin animals. It is quiet but smart. It is fluid in its movements. It likes to fight in close. It has power and techniques that you don't expect. When it gets knocked down, it springs back.

You will either succeed or end up being the toughest opponent most will ever meet. Everything starts happening right now!

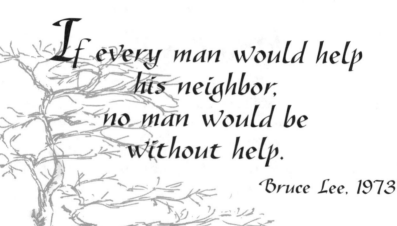

*If every man would help
his neighbor,
no man would be
without help.*

Bruce Lee, 1973

83
Pass Along The Secret

Following the Shaolin way, being kind and patient and prosperous and generous, you will find your counsel being sought by many. They will want to know how they can find the *do*, the way.

The secret to share with them is to stop looking for secrets that don't exist. Most already know the way to success. Is it persistence and determination and hard work and having clearly defined goals which are broken down into manageable objectives? It is. Is it the Golden Rule, which is doing to others as you would have them do unto you? It is. Most of us know it. As a follower of the Shaolin, you act on it.

Forget injuries,
never forget
kindnesses.

Chinese proverb

84
Give Generously

Follow the principles of the Shaolin and you will be blessed with much more than you need. You will work hard towards your goals and you will be liked. Just these two attributes will result in your being well rewarded. Your organizational abilities will give you more time than most. Your persistence and determination will get you more financial reward than most. You must earn before you can give. Share your time and money. Send lots of flowers, candy, e-mails, teddy bears and thank yous. Be generous and then forget it.

Selflessly, share your time and money because it is right. In the martial arts, the giving of a gift is called *giri* and *giri* creates a burden to respond. You will set in motion a chain of positive actions and reactions. See GIVE FREELY #24.

To see what is right and
not to do it is
to want of courage.

Confucius, 551–479 B.C.

85
Build A Business

To provide for yourself and your family and society, you need time and money. Think in terms of being an entrepreneur or an intrapreneur. An entrepreneur is a self-reliant person who owns his own business. An intrapreneur is a valued employee who works for a company but acts like an entrepreneur: finding new ways, encouraging co-workers, working hard, etc.

The business that you are in doesn't matter. You can run a karate *dojo*, be a painter, sell insurance or provide consulting services. For all businesses, the rules are the same. You must offer a quality product or service at a fair price. You must appreciate your customer. Research your industry. Stay well informed regarding current events and trade developments. You will find others who have already done or are doing what you want to do and you can do what they are doing or have done. In the beginning, be more imitative than innovative. If you read a thousand business books, you will see the value in these simple rules. Just follow the leaders to success.

For more information about starting and succeeding at business, take the Winning With Small Business Course at www.success.org. It's all FREE.

To listen well is as powerful a means of influence as to talk well, and is as essential to all true conversation.

Chinese proverb

86
Develop Your Special Talent

You were born with a special talent. It may be to sing, dance, write, teach, paint, sculpt, mentor, volunteer, preach, defend, pray, lead, coach, plant, rescue or befriend. It's something. You have something special to offer the world. There is something that you can do better than 10,000 other people. You must keep learning and trying new things to find your special talent. The world needs your gift.

By following the Shaolin principles, you will get prosperous enough soon enough that you will have time left in your life to be the special you. Here is a hint. The special you will involve offering something of benefit to others.

To become different from
what we are,
we must have some
awareness of
what we are.

Bruce Lee, 1975,
Tao of Jeet Kune Do

176

87
Appreciate Your Appeal

Following the Shaolin principles and being a warrior-monk makes you an appealing, charismatic person. When you are appealing, students will want to learn from you, bosses will want to promote you, banks will want to lend you money and customers will want to buy your products or services. You will be charming.

Your allure to others will be your genuine selflessness in wanting to help them to achieve their objective, whether that is to become a black belt or buy a car.

By not trying to be a salesperson but rather a true customer service person, you will make more sales. By teaching karate and showing your students how good they can be rather than how great you are, you will attract more students.

Charisma isn't painted on the outside. It comes from the inside. Charisma says: *I like you and I want to help you.* With this attitude, you stand to be liked by many.

Do you need proof
of God?
Does one light a torch
to see the Sun?

Japanese proverb

88
Remember These Words

Taxpayer, homeowner, graduate, veteran, champion, employer, investor, citizen, defender, churchgoer, volunteer, reader, teacher, friend, ambassador, guardian, scholar, peacemaker, musician, artist, host, believer, monk, entrepreneur, owner, representative, neighbor, warrior, parent, employee, philanthropist, helper, black belt, partner, intrapreneur, leader, activist, player, worker. These are good things to be.

Self-education makes great men.

Bruce Lee, 1973

89
Teach Yourself

You are responsible for your own education. When you want to learn about a new subject, go to the library. Go to the bookstores and buy books and magazines. Log on to the Internet. Join a club or association. Find experts in the field. Ask questions and more questions. Take courses and ask your teacher questions. Don't just sit there. Make the course your course.

What do you want to know about the martial arts? All you can. What do you want to know about your business? Everything you can.

Hunger for knowledge because knowledge is power. You don't need to attend famous universities. You don't need a lot of money for tuitions. By yourself, with your own free will, you can learn anything that you want to learn. Learning is a gift that you give yourself. Knowledge is portable. You take it with you everywhere.

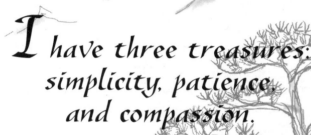

I have three treasures:
simplicity, patience,
and compassion.

Tao Te Ching, 67

90
Form Your Day

You greet the new day with a positive mental attitude knowing that today brings you one day closer to your goals.

You have a written to-do list which you have prioritized.

Today you will exercise, eat sensibly and find twenty minutes for your personal quiet time.

You will act as someone that you would admire. You are friendly and in control.

You will perform both planned and random acts of kindness.

You will do something nice just for yourself today.

You will endeavor to learn something new today.

You will stop at times to appreciate small things.

You will plan a bright and successful tomorrow.

*The superior man
has a dignified ease
without pride.
The common man
has pride without
dignified ease.*

Confucius, 551–479 B.C.

91
Do What Others Can't

Most people can't give two nights a month to volunteer at a hospice. You can.

Most people can't get up at 6:00 AM and jog two miles. You can.

Most people can't give up half of their lunch hour to solve a customer's problem. You can.

Most people can't help to clean up other people's messes. You can.

Most people can't help a friend deal with destructive behavior. You can.

Most people can't give five percent of their money to charity. You can.

You can. You are of the Shaolin.

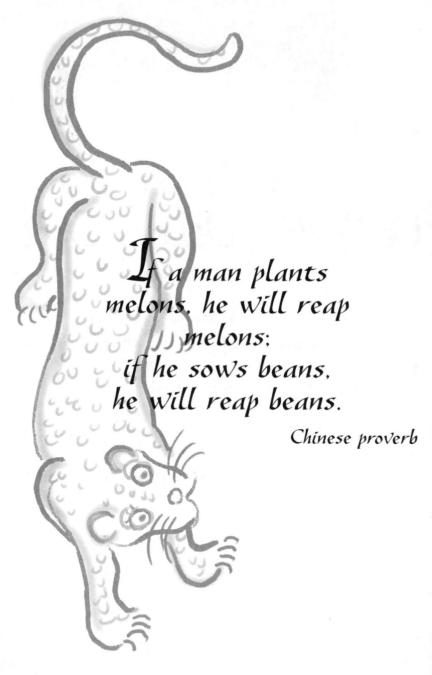

If a man plants
melons, he will reap
melons;
if he sows beans,
he will reap beans.

Chinese proverb

92
Build Upon Your Basics

To become an effective martial artist, you must start from a strong foundation of basics. Work on your front, back and thrust punches. Work on your front and side kicks. Work on your 8-point blocking system. Work on your movements in your *katas*. Work on your balance and breathing. Your basics form a complete fighting style. Everything else is icing on the cake.

To be a successful businessperson, you must start from a strong foundation of basics. Offer a quality product or service at a fair price. Appreciate your customer. Keep improving your products, services and customer service. These basics form a complete business plan. Everything else is icing on the cake.

Nothingness cannot be defined; the softest thing cannot be snapped.

Bruce Lee, 1975,
Tao of Jeet Kune Do

93
Avoid Thinking That

... you are too young or too old or too weak or haven't got the time to become a black belt and enjoy the rewards of the Shaolin. You can do it.

... chanting or fasting are necessary to find yourself. They aren't.

... you need a lot of money to start a business. You can start most businesses small or part-time.

... you need more than eight hours sleep. Get up.

... you need a personal trainer to exercise. Start walking.

... you need advanced university degrees to be successful. You can pick and choose courses as needed. You can educate yourself.

... planning, hard work, generosity and persistence won't get you anywhere. They will.

... you have to work forty or fifty years before retirement. You probably don't.

... the world owes you anything. It doesn't.

A military operation involves deception. Even though you are competent, appear to be incompetent. Though effective, appear to be ineffective.

Sun-tzu, 400 B.C.,
The Art of War

94
Be The Monk

Be known as: youthful, successful, controlled, powerful, loyal, passionate, vital, noble, courteous, competent, confident, strong, polite, spiritual, cheerful, generous, honest, happy, kind, modest, centered, secure, disciplined, imaginative, capable, dynamic, motivating, calm, decent, fit, serene, romantic, charismatic, able, daring, diplomatic, patient, inspiring, courageous, vibrant, captivating, altruistic, cultured, clean, funny, enterprising, compassionate, brave, creative, prosperous, persistent, robust, charming, joyous, determined, sophisticated, respectful, hard working, humble, positive, active, thrifty, appealing, delightful, warm, chivalrous, considerate, frugal, unselfish, optimistic, affluent, peaceful, loving, diligent, curious, bold, tenacious, faithful, educated, principled, energetic and elegant. Establish your reputation. See BE THE WARRIOR #15.

*Let the past drift away
with the water.*

Japanese proverb

95
Use The Power of Patience

You can handle most problems because you know from following the Shaolin way, that only a little bit of time stands between you and your goal.

It may take twenty calls to make a sale. Be patient. It might take you five attempts to quit smoking or drugs or lose weight. It might take ten applications to get the job you really want. The point is that you will try and keep trying until you succeed. You must take that first step. Most people quit too soon. Be persistent. Be patient.

All the jobs and all the houses and all the world's treasures eventually pass from old hands to young. Wait. Your time is coming.

Concentrate on your major goal until you have achieved it.

A peasant must stand for a long time on a hillside with his mouth open before a roast duck flies in.

Chinese proverb

194

96
Develop Your Sense Of Humor

In all areas of life, a quick wit, a hearty laugh, a smile and a warm sense of humor are appreciated. To be a good joke teller, tell jokes often. It's just practice and it's modeling your delivery after comedians you admire and funny friends you know. Start a joke file.

Always be absolutely sure that your material is clean and non-offensive. Stick to a universally funny subject - you. You will learn that most of the best humor is self-deprecating. That is, you have to learn to laugh at yourself. On your road to success, there will be many stumbles and fumbles providing many opportunities for you to turn the unexpected into stress-reducing laughter. Don't sweat the small stuff. Laugh about it. Be affable. Humor will add to your attractiveness.

*Control your emotion or
it will control you.*

Chinese proverb

97
Control Conflict

You are the monk. Remain calm and detached. Allow the other party to rage while you consider the appropriate response. Should you reason, agree, apologize, fight or leave? Which is to your benefit and to the benefit of those you must protect?

Let go of your anger. It only clouds the issue and draws you into a quick response. Temper anger with kindness. Kindness is a weapon against evil. Neutralize shouting with soft words. Answer threats with serene confidence. Breathe deeply with short inhales and long exhales. Let the anger wash over you. Maintain your presence. Don't exaggerate. Don't lie.

Attempt to be an active peacemaker, building bridges of understanding and negotiating win-win solutions.

What you do not want done to yourself, do not do to others.

Confucius, 551–479 B.C.

98
Take The Punch

If you watch a boxing or a karate match, you will notice that few contests end without a heated exchange of blows. Even the eventual winner may take many punches before victory. In going from white belt to black belt, you will take your share of punches. This is expected.

In business, going from few assets to financial independence, you can also expect to take your share of punches in the form of personal rejection. *"May I mow your lawn?" "No."* Intentional or not, this rejection can be a personal blow to your ego. Most people will retreat to the comfort zone and do everything possible to avoid personal rejection. Knocking on doors and making cold calls is the best way to get new customers but when making any type of direct appeal, you face personal rejection. Some will listen to your offer and say: *No.* Many won't even listen. You make the next call.

It is easier, yet so much less effective, to hide behind impersonal print, radio, or TV advertising. Of course, advertising has an important role to play in business success but to get to where you want to go, you have to risk making personal requests and taking your share of punches. On the road to YES, there are frequently many NOs.

Every self-made person will have a repertoire of stories of the fights and punches they took and continue to endure. These are the war stories. This is what makes final victory so satisfying.

When it comes to establishing rules and regulations, everyone high and low, should be treated alike.

Sun-tzu, 400 B.C.,
The Art of War

99
Become Grateful

Life isn't exactly the way you want it to be. You will have your ups and downs and crosses to bear. You will have plenty of opportunities to practice holding your tongue and exercising patience. Yet, because your eyes are focused on the larger picture, you will be able to keep everyday events in their proper perspective.

In the larger scheme of things, you may wish to be grateful for good health, a supportive spouse, a rewarding profession, obedient children, conscientious employees, prosperity, religious faith, loyal friends and even winning sport teams. You add and choose.

When you can look forward and be thankful, you can help others in your charge to do the same. Hold the burning candle from which others can light their candles.

This is the discipline of Shaolin.

I hear and I forget,
I see and I remember, I do
and I understand.

Chinese proverb

100
Rejoice In The Day

You got up early. You did your best at work. You exercised your mind and body. You were pleasant to others. You did a good deed. You took time to reflect and plan tomorrow. Now, take pleasure in your accomplishments of this day. Be proud of yourself. If you keep putting days like this together, there is no telling how far you will go and how many lives you will be able to touch in a positive way. Today, you moved one day closer to achieving your goals.

To Help Others, We Need Your Help

If you share the philosophy behind these action principles and would like to assist us in our work, here is your opportunity. Be a person of action. We need your financial support to carry on our work. If you are a student or a would-be entrepreneur, a small donation would be appropriate. If you are a successful businessperson for whom these action principles have played a significant role and you want others to benefit, you'll want to do much more. Please call 1-800-585-1300 with your credit card donation or send your donation to us at 5 North Main Street, Natick, MA 01760. You can also make a contribution via our website at www.success.org. The American Success Institute is a 501(c)3 nonprofit organization and donations are tax deductible. Please verify your particular situation with your accountant.

We thank you in advance for your generosity.

How To Use Our Publications

The American Success Institute publishes a series of pocket-sized motivational books. Purchasing and distributing these books as a businessperson or an individual will show your commitment to positive living.

Some people will use the books as their business cards. You can staple your regular business card onto the cover or you can stamp your name and business information to an inside page. Give the books to new prospects or use them as premiums for existing customers.

You can purchase our books and donate them to local social service or religious organizations, or to schools and libraries. This can be your way of expressing your gratitude to your community.

If you represent a nonprofit organization, you can purchase and resell these little books as a fundraising tool.

By purchasing these books, you help support the work of the American Success Institute to help motivate individuals to realize their potential through self-reliance.

Join us. Be a part of this important motivational work.

Publications
How to order

The American Success Institute (ASI) publishes a number of pocket-sized motivational books. Books are sold in blocks of 10 for $15.00 plus $4.50 shipping and handling. MA residents please add 5% Sales Tax. Single copies are $6.00 including shipping and handling.

Current titles:

- *Positive Mental Attitudes*
- *100 Action Principles of the Shaolin*
- *Tenga una actitud mental positiva (Spanish)*
- *African-Americans on Success*
- *Women on Success*
- *Sports Legends on Success*
- *101 Questions and Answers on Small Business*

Mail orders should be sent to:

ASI, 5 North Main Street, Natick, MA 01760

To order books with a credit card: 1-800-585-1300

Help us to help you help others.

Shaolin Master™ Products

100 Action Principles of the Shaolin

- Pocket-Sized - One Copy FREE (Available ONLY by completing order form at www.success.org/free)

- Additional Pocket-Sized Copies $1.50 (Distributed ONLY in blocks of 10 copies for $15 plus $4.50 s/h.)

- Pocket-Sized Copy - Autographed by Bill $10.00 plus $3.00 s/h.

- Deluxe Edition with motivational quotes $12.95 plus $3.00 s/h.

- Deluxe Edition - Autographed by Bill $20.00 plus $3.00 s/h.

- Limited Edition - Genuine Leather - Autographed by Bill - Any donation to ASI of $100.

- Audio Edition - 2 tapes or CD - $20.00 plus $3.00 s/h.

* Deluxe Edition (Spanish version) with motivational quotes $12.95 plus $3.00 s/h.

* Video tapes of Bill's Shaolin Master™ television program - $20.00 plus $3.00 s/h.

*Shaolin Music CD - Soothing guitar music with an Oriental flavor - $20.00 plus $3.00 s/h.

*Check www.success.org for availability of these items.

To order: Call 1-800-585-1300

The American Success Institute is a 501 (c)3 nonprofit educational and publishing organization. Our principal teaching is done through our national award-winning website at www.success.org. The mission of ASI is to foster positive values resulting in economic self-sufficiency.

American Success Institute
5 North Main Street
Natick, MA 01760

www.success.org

Phone: 508-651-3303

e-mail: info@success.org

Notes

Notes

Notes

Notes

Notes

Notes

Notes